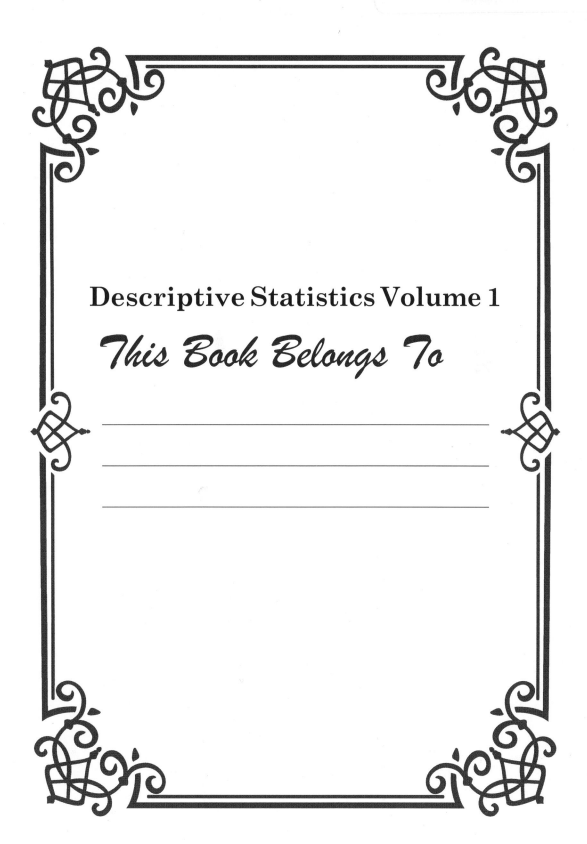

Descriptive Statistics Volume 1

This Book Belongs To

_____

_____

_____

1 A farmer has 70 lambs, 180 cats, 170 pigs, 130 sheep, 120 cows and 330 horses.
Represent the data by a pie chart in percentage.

2 Mr. XYZ monthly income is $3450. The monthly expenses of his family on various items are given below.
$850 on education, $750 on internet, $850 on taxes and $1000 on clothing.
Represent the data by a pie chart in percentage.

3 Various modes of transport used by 1000 students in a given college are given below.
220 car, 190 motorbike, 110 train, 180 bus and 300 bicycle.
Represent the data by a pie chart in percentage.

4 The number of different fruits kept in a large basket are given below.
47 lemons, 45 apples, 23 oranges, 33 strawberries, 42 pomegranates and 10 pears.
Represent the data by a pie chart in percentage.

5 A farmer has 310 turkeys, 310 goats, 360 horses and 430 cats.
Represent the data by a pie chart in percentage.

6 Mr. XYZ monthly income is $8750. The monthly expenses of his family on various items are given below.
$1900 on clothing, $1700 on taxes, $2000 on insurance, $850 on toiletries and $2300 on rent.
Represent the data by a pie chart in percentage.

7 Various modes of transport used by 1410 students in a given college are given below.
120 motorbike, 190 boat, 340 bicycle, 440 on foot, 220 subway and 100 train.
Represent the data by a pie chart in percentage.

8 The number of different fruits kept in a large basket are given below.
34 lemons, 30 pomegranates, 27 oranges and 48 coconuts.
Represent the data by a pic chart in percentage.

9 A farmer has 230 pigs, 350 chickens, 130 cats, 200 hens and 320 roosters.
Represent the data by a pie chart in percentage.

10 Mr. XYZ monthly income is $8250. The monthly expenses of his family on various items are given below.
$1350 on food, $2400 on education, $800 on internet, $1900 on taxes, $900 on savings and $900 on haircut.
Represent the data by a pie chart in percentage.

11 Various modes of transport used by 1210 students in a given college are given below.
280 motorbike, 270 bus, 310 train and 350 car.
Represent the data by a pie chart in percentage.

12 The number of different fruits kept in a large basket are given below.
10 pears, 33 cherries, 10 apples, 10 lemons and 23 coconuts.
Represent the data by a pie chart in percentage.

13 A farmer has 80 geese, 280 chickens, 300 pigs, 310 cats, 120 ducks and 440 dogs.
Represent the data by a pie chart in percentage.

14 Mr. XYZ monthly income is $7600. The monthly expenses of his family on various items are given below.
$1450 on toiletries, $2050 on gas, $2000 on clothing and $2100 on insurance.
Represent the data by a pie chart in percentage.

15 Various modes of transport used by 1180 students in a given college are given below.
280 car, 150 bus, 210 subway, 100 bicycle and 440 train.
Represent the data by a pie chart in percentage.

16 The number of different fruits kept in a large basket are given below.
12 strawberries, 7 lemons, 34 apples, 31 pears, 21 oranges and 11 cherries.
Represent the data by a pie chart in percentage.

17 A farmer has 330 geese, 290 lambs, 480 rabbits and 370 sheep.
Represent the data by a pie chart in percentage.

18 Mr. XYZ monthly income is $5900. The monthly expenses of his family on various items are given below.
$1400 on gas, $1200 on medication, $750 on insurance, $950 on taxes and $1600 on internet.
Represent the data by a pie chart in percentage.

19 Various modes of transport used by 1710 students in a given college are given below.
390 boat, 280 bus, 260 car, 270 motorbike, 380 train and 130 on foot.
Represent the data by a pie chart in percentage.

20 The number of different fruits kept in a large basket are given below.
20 apples, 26 strawberries, 19 pomegranates and 27 pears.
Represent the data by a pie chart in percentage.

21 A farmer has 260 horses, 290 geese, 440 roosters, 120 cats and 200 hens.
Represent the data by a pie chart in percentage.

22 Mr. XYZ monthly income is $10200. The monthly expenses of his family on various items are given below.
$2300 on rent, $2350 on gas, $1050 on savings, $2400 on taxes, $750 on food and $1350 on toiletries.
Represent the data by a pie chart in percentage.

23 Various modes of transport used by 1160 students in a given college are given below.
270 motorbike, 190 car, 360 train and 340 on foot.
Represent the data by a pie chart in percentage.

24 The number of different fruits kept in a large basket are given below.
25 pears, 49 bananas, 19 cherries, 35 apples and 7 lemons.
Represent the data by a pie chart in percentage.

25 A farmer has 300 cats, 330 pigs, 80 dogs, 100 hens, 190 roosters and 380 ducks.
Represent the data by a pie chart in percentage.

26 Mr. XYZ monthly income is $5100. The monthly expenses of his family on various items are given below.
$1050 on medication, $1400 on education, $1200 on haircut and $1450 on savings.
Represent the data by a pie chart in percentage.

27 Various modes of transport used by 1400 students in a given college are given below.
320 subway, 250 boat, 460 bicycle, 260 on foot and 110 car.
Represent the data by a pie chart in percentage.

28 The number of different fruits kept in a large basket are given below.
41 apples, 39 pears, 18 coconuts, 34 grapes, 14 lemons and 19 pomegranates.
Represent the data by a pie chart in percentage.

29 A farmer has 250 hens, 380 geese, 320 lambs and 460 cats.
Represent the data by a pie chart in percentage.

30 Mr. XYZ monthly income is $8200. The monthly expenses of his family on various items are given below.
$550 on haircut, $1250 on medication, $2100 on gas, $2150 on education and $2150 on food.
Represent the data by a pie chart in percentage.

31 Various modes of transport used by 1540 students in a given college are given below.
360 motorbike, 320 bicycle, 250 boat, 240 subway, 290 car and 80 on foot.
Represent the data by a pie chart in percentage.

32 The number of different fruits kept in a large basket are given below.
30 apples, 49 mangoes, 45 oranges and 49 bananas.
Represent the data by a pie chart in percentage.

33 A farmer has 390 roosters, 390 donkeys, 470 pigs, 290 turkeys and 150 cows.
Represent the data by a pie chart in percentage.

34 Mr. XYZ monthly income is $8450. The monthly expenses of his family on various items are given below.

$550 on savings, $1600 on taxes, $1700 on gas, $2250 on medication, $1600 on toiletries and $750 on food.

Represent the data by a pie chart in percentage.

35 Various modes of transport used by 1300 students in a given college are given below.

160 boat, 460 motorbike, 280 bus and 400 on foot.

Represent the data by a pie chart in percentage.

36 The number of different fruits kept in a large basket are given below.

14 pears, 17 grapes, 34 bananas, 39 apples and 42 pomegranates.

Represent the data by a pie chart in percentage.

37 A farmer has 130 hens, 370 roosters, 330 donkeys, 210 lambs, 290 pigs and 450 rabbits.

Represent the data by a pie chart in percentage.

38 Mr. XYZ monthly income is $5100. The monthly expenses of his family on various items are given below.

$750 on insurance, $1750 on savings, $1100 on gas and $1500 on rent.

Represent the data by a pie chart in percentage.

39 Various modes of transport used by 940 students in a given college are given below.

90 on foot, 170 car, 130 subway, 210 bus and 340 train.

Represent the data by a pie chart in percentage.

40 The number of different fruits kept in a large basket are given below.

11 cherries, 12 oranges, 38 pomegranates, 39 pears, 18 coconuts and 13 apples.

Represent the data by a pie chart in percentage.

41 A farmer has 310 hens, 310 dogs, 350 sheep and 480 cows.

Represent the data by a pie chart in percentage.

42 Mr. XYZ monthly income is $6250. The monthly expenses of his family on various items are given below.

$700 on clothing, $900 on food, $1300 on savings, $1400 on toiletries and $1950 on insurance.

Represent the data by a pie chart in percentage.

43 Various modes of transport used by 1140 students in a given college are given below.

280 bicycle, 280 on foot, 60 train, 210 car, 240 motorbike and 70 subway.

Represent the data by a pie chart in percentage.

44 The number of different fruits kept in a large basket are given below.
29 grapes, 26 cherries, 34 strawberries and 34 pomegranates.
Represent the data by a pie chart in percentage.

45 A farmer has 100 ducks, 210 hens, 260 cows, 220 rabbits and 470 donkeys.
Represent the data by a pie chart in percentage.

46 Mr. XYZ monthly income is $6900. The monthly expenses of his family on various items are given below.
$900 on rent, $800 on food, $1750 on taxes, $650 on gas, $950 on insurance and $1850 on medication.
Represent the data by a pie chart in percentage.

47 Various modes of transport used by 1140 students in a given college are given below.
190 bus, 310 subway, 350 bicycle and 290 boat.
Represent the data by a pie chart in percentage.

48 The number of different fruits kept in a large basket are given below.
9 pears, 30 cherries, 20 lemons, 13 pomegranates and 8 oranges.
Represent the data by a pie chart in percentage.

49 A farmer has 230 cats, 90 chickens, 430 lambs, 330 hens, 90 ducks and 490 pigs.
Represent the data by a pie chart in percentage.

50 Mr. XYZ monthly income is $5200. The monthly expenses of his family on various items are given below.
$1150 on taxes, $1300 on gas, $1350 on savings and $1400 on medication.
Represent the data by a pie chart in percentage.

51 Various modes of transport used by 1790 students in a given college are given below.
420 bus, 290 bicycle, 180 motorbike, 410 car and 490 train.
Represent the data by a pie chart in percentage.

52 The number of different fruits kept in a large basket are given below.
23 strawberries, 47 pears, 8 bananas, 23 oranges, 20 pomegranates and 9 grapes.
Represent the data by a pie chart in percentage.

53 A farmer has 170 sheep, 320 dogs, 120 chickens and 320 turkeys.
Represent the data by a pie chart in percentage.

54 Mr. XYZ monthly income is $6000. The monthly expenses of his family on various items are given below.
$1400 on medication, $1050 on haircut, $2300 on gas, $550 on insurance and $700 on education.
Represent the data by a pie chart in percentage.

55 Various modes of transport used by 1610 students in a given college are given below.
370 subway, 410 bus, 250 train, 120 bicycle, 350 boat and 110 car.
Represent the data by a pie chart in percentage.

56 The number of different fruits kept in a large basket are given below.
13 lemons, 48 mangoes, 17 oranges and 37 pomegranates.
Represent the data by a pie chart in percentage.

57 A farmer has 370 cats, 300 cows, 300 pigs, 110 rabbits and 480 chickens.
Represent the data by a pie chart in percentage.

58 Mr. XYZ monthly income is $10550. The monthly expenses of his family on various items are given below.
$2350 on haircut, $2100 on food, $600 on clothing, $2400 on medication, $2100 on education and $1000 on rent.
Represent the data by a pie chart in percentage.

59 Various modes of transport used by 1000 students in a given college are given below.
90 subway, 450 motorbike, 140 car and 320 train.
Represent the data by a pie chart in percentage.

60 The number of different fruits kept in a large basket are given below.
32 bananas, 44 cherries, 26 lemons, 17 pears and 47 mangoes.
Represent the data by a pie chart in percentage.

61 A farmer has 370 cats, 440 horses, 160 roosters, 170 donkeys, 300 chickens and 140 dogs.
Represent the data by a pie chart in percentage.

62 Mr. XYZ monthly income is $6050. The monthly expenses of his family on various items are given below.
$1000 on clothing, $2200 on gas, $750 on internet and $2100 on haircut.
Represent the data by a pie chart in percentage.

63 Various modes of transport used by 1420 students in a given college are given below.
180 train, 120 motorbike, 370 boat, 300 on foot and 450 bus.
Represent the data by a pie chart in percentage.

64 The number of different fruits kept in a large basket are given below.
16 apples, 20 bananas, 21 lemons, 10 strawberries, 16 mangoes and 47 oranges.
Represent the data by a pie chart in percentage.

65 A farmer has 380 cats, 450 lambs, 380 cows and 460 roosters.
Represent the data by a pie chart in percentage.

66 Calculate mean, median, mode and bar chart based on the following table, where n_i denotes the absolute frequency of each value x_i:

x_i	n_i
10	4
18	6
26	3
34	8

67 Calculate mean, median, mode and bar chart based on the following table, where n_i denotes the absolute frequency of each value x_i:

x_i	n_i
17	3
25	8
33	5
41	6

68 Calculate mean, median, mode and bar chart based on the following table, where n_i denotes the absolute frequency of each value x_i:

x_i	n_i
13	4
16	7
19	8
22	1

69 Calculate mean, median, mode and bar chart based on the following table, where n_i denotes the absolute frequency of each value x_i:

x_i	n_i
0	3
4	2
8	6
12	4

70 Calculate mean, median, mode and bar chart based on the following table, where n_i denotes the absolute frequency of each value x_i:

x_i	n_i
8	5
12	6
16	7
20	1

71 Calculate mean, median, mode and bar chart based on the following table, where n_i denotes the absolute frequency of each value x_i:

x_i	n_i
0	2
4	9
8	4
12	3

72 Calculate mean, median, mode and bar chart based on the following table, where n_i denotes the absolute frequency of each value x_i:

x_i	n_i
20	4
26	7
32	1
38	8

73 Calculate mean, median, mode and bar chart based on the following table, where n_i denotes the absolute frequency of each value x_i:

x_i	n_i
0	7
8	6
16	5
24	2

74 Calculate mean, median, mode and bar chart based on the following table, where n_i denotes the absolute frequency of each value x_i:

x_i	n_i
17	4
19	5
21	8
23	7

75 Calculate mean, median, mode and bar chart based on the following table, where n_i denotes the absolute frequency of each value x_i:

x_i	n_i
19	3
25	8
31	5
37	1

76 Calculate mean, median, mode and bar chart based on the following table, where n_i denotes the absolute frequency of each value x_i:

x_i	n_i
22	2
24	6
26	9
28	7

77 Calculate mean, median, mode and bar chart based on the following table, where n_i denotes the absolute frequency of each value x_i:

x_i	n_i
33	9
40	3
47	5
54	4

78 Calculate mean, median, mode and bar chart based on the following table, where n_i denotes the absolute frequency of each value x_i:

x_i	n_i
0	5
10	4
20	2
30	6

79 Calculate mean, median, mode and bar chart based on the following table, where n_i denotes the absolute frequency of each value x_i:

x_i	n_i
33	4
39	1
45	6
51	3

80 Calculate mean, median, mode and bar chart based on the following table, where n_i denotes the absolute frequency of each value x_i:

x_i	n_i
29	9
37	2
45	4
53	5

81 Calculate mean, median, mode and bar chart based on the following table, where n_i denotes the absolute frequency of each value x_i:

x_i	n_i
32	8
36	7
40	2
44	4

82 Calculate mean, median, mode and bar chart based on the following table, where n_i denotes the absolute frequency of each value x_i:

x_i	n_i
38	8
47	4
56	3
65	2

83 Calculate mean, median, mode and bar chart based on the following table, where n_i denotes the absolute frequency of each value x_i:

x_i	n_i
15	5
22	2
29	4
36	6

84 Calculate mean, median, mode and bar chart based on the following table, where n_i denotes the absolute frequency of each value x_i:

x_i	n_i
12	8
14	5
16	1
18	4

85 Calculate mean, median, mode and bar chart based on the following table, where n_i denotes the absolute frequency of each value x_i:

x_i	n_i
20	2
30	8
40	7
50	4

86 Calculate mean, median, mode and bar chart based on the following table, where n_i denotes the absolute frequency of each value x_i:

x_i	n_i
0	7
9	3
18	6
27	5

87 Calculate mean, median, mode and bar chart based on the following table, where n_i denotes the absolute frequency of each value x_i:

x_i	n_i
23	1
26	2
29	4
32	3

88 Calculate mean, median, mode and bar chart based on the following table, where n_i denotes the absolute frequency of each value x_i:

x_i	n_i
23	5
33	7
43	2
53	4
63	6

89 Calculate mean, median, mode and bar chart based on the following table, where n_i denotes the absolute frequency of each value x_i:

x_i	n_i
34	3
43	2
52	1
61	8
70	6

90 Calculate mean, median, mode and bar chart based on the following table, where n_i denotes the absolute frequency of each value x_i:

x_i	n_i
17	5
22	3
27	6
32	9
37	2

91 Calculate mean, median, mode and bar chart based on the following table, where n_i denotes the absolute frequency of each value x_i:

x_i	n_i
21	3
22	9
23	2
24	6
25	4

92 Calculate mean, median, mode and bar chart based on the following table, where n_i denotes the absolute frequency of each value x_i:

x_i	n_i
11	5
19	1
27	3
35	6
43	2

93 Calculate mean, median, mode and bar chart based on the following table, where n_i denotes the absolute frequency of each value x_i:

x_i	n_i
0	8
6	3
12	2
18	7
24	4

13

94 Calculate mean, median, mode and bar chart based on the following table, where n_i denotes the absolute frequency of each value x_i:

x_i	n_i
20	3
24	8
28	2
32	6
36	1

95 Calculate mean, median, mode and bar chart based on the following table, where n_i denotes the absolute frequency of each value x_i:

x_i	n_i
31	2
34	3
37	8
40	6
43	7

96 Calculate mean, median, mode and bar chart based on the following table, where n_i denotes the absolute frequency of each value x_i:

x_i	n_i
4	8
6	1
8	3
10	2
12	7

97 Calculate mean, median, mode and bar chart based on the following table, where n_i denotes the absolute frequency of each value x_i:

x_i	n_i
23	6
30	7
37	4
44	5
51	9

98 Calculate mean, median, mode and bar chart based on the following table, where n_i denotes the absolute frequency of each value x_i:

x_i	n_i
6	4
10	6
14	3
18	7
22	9

99 Calculate mean, median, mode and bar chart based on the following table, where n_i denotes the absolute frequency of each value x_i:

x_i	n_i
11	2
12	4
13	6
14	3
15	1

100 Calculate mean, median, mode and bar chart based on the following table, where n_i denotes the absolute frequency of each value x_i:

x_i	n_i
5	3
9	7
13	8
17	1
21	2

101 Calculate mean, median, mode and bar chart based on the following table, where n_i denotes the absolute frequency of each value x_i:

x_i	n_i
28	4
32	1
36	3
40	6
44	5

102 Calculate mean, median, mode and bar chart based on the following table, where n_i denotes the absolute frequency of each value x_i:

x_i	n_i
0	8
8	5
16	4
24	3
32	6

103 Calculate mean, median, mode and bar chart based on the following table, where n_i denotes the absolute frequency of each value x_i:

x_i	n_i
24	1
27	6
30	8
33	5
36	2

104 Calculate mean, median, mode and bar chart based on the following table, where n_i denotes the absolute frequency of each value x_i:

x_i	n_i
27	8
35	2
43	6
51	4
59	5

105 Calculate mean, median, mode and bar chart based on the following table, where n_i denotes the absolute frequency of each value x_i:

x_i	n_i
0	3
6	2
12	4
18	7
24	9

106 Calculate mean, median, mode and bar chart based on the following table, where n_i denotes the absolute frequency of each value x_i:

x_i	n_i
4	4
7	2
10	8
13	6
16	3

107 Calculate mean, median, mode and bar chart based on the following table, where n_i denotes the absolute frequency of each value x_i:

x_i	n_i
36	8
44	5
52	1
60	3
68	6

108 Calculate mean, median, mode and bar chart based on the following table, where n_i denotes the absolute frequency of each value x_i:

x_i	n_i
26	8
30	7
34	5
38	2
42	6

109 Calculate mean, median, mode and bar chart based on the following table, where n_i denotes the absolute frequency of each value x_i:

x_i	n_i
30	6
33	9
36	2
39	7
42	4

110 Calculate mean, median, mode and bar chart based on the following table, where n_i denotes the absolute frequency of each value x_i:

x_i	n_i
25	5
33	8
41	2
49	9
57	7
65	4

111 Calculate mean, median, mode and bar chart based on the following table, where n_i denotes the absolute frequency of each value x_i:

x_i	n_i
32	5
39	9
46	7
53	6
60	3
67	8

112 Calculate mean, median, mode and bar chart based on the following table, where n_i denotes the absolute frequency of each value x_i:

x_i	n_i
22	1
24	6
26	7
28	2
30	3
32	8

113 Calculate mean, median, mode and bar chart based on the following table, where n_i denotes the absolute frequency of each value x_i:

x_i	n_i
0	9
3	5
6	6
9	7
12	8
15	3

114 Calculate mean, median, mode and bar chart based on the following table, where n_i denotes the absolute frequency of each value x_i:

x_i	n_i
0	5
4	7
8	2
12	6
16	3
20	4

115 Calculate mean, median, mode and bar chart based on the following table, where n_i denotes the absolute frequency of each value x_i:

x_i	n_i
27	3
33	2
39	8
45	1
51	4
57	6

116 Calculate mean, median, mode and bar chart based on the following table, where n_i denotes the absolute frequency of each value x_i:

x_i	n_i
0	2
4	1
8	5
12	8
16	4
20	3

117 Calculate mean, median, mode and bar chart based on the following table, where n_i denotes the absolute frequency of each value x_i:

x_i	n_i
0	9
2	4
4	7
6	8
8	3
10	6

118 Calculate mean, median, mode and bar chart based on the following table, where n_i denotes the absolute frequency of each value x_i:

x_i	n_i
29	5
32	1
35	6
38	9
41	2
44	8

119 Calculate mean, median, mode and bar chart based on the following table, where n_i denotes the absolute frequency of each value x_i:

x_i	n_i
~~20~~	~~2~~
26	9
32	3
38	4
44	7
50	8

120 Calculate mean, median, mode and bar chart based on the following table, where n_i denotes the absolute frequency of each value x_i:

x_i	n_i
0	5
9	4
18	1
27	2
36	8
45	6

121 Calculate mean, median, mode and bar chart based on the following table, where n_i denotes the absolute frequency of each value x_i:

x_i	n_i
0	2
2	7
4	3
6	4
8	5
10	1

122 Calculate mean, median, mode and bar chart based on the following table, where n_i denotes the absolute frequency of each value x_i:

x_i	n_i
25	8
28	3
31	2
34	4
37	5
40	1

123 Calculate mean, median, mode and bar chart based on the following table, where n_i denotes the absolute frequency of each value x_i:

x_i	n_i
16	2
21	9
26	8
31	6
36	7
41	4

124 Calculate mean, median, mode and bar chart based on the following table, where n_i denotes the absolute frequency of each value x_i:

x_i	n_i
34	5
39	1
44	9
49	6
54	7
59	2

125 Calculate mean, median, mode and bar chart based on the following table, where n_i denotes the absolute frequency of each value x_i:

x_i	n_i
25	7
34	3
43	4
52	2
61	9
70	6

126 Calculate mean, median, mode and bar chart based on the following table, where n_i denotes the absolute frequency of each value x_i:

x_i	n_i
0	8
8	5
16	6
24	2
32	3
40	4

127 Calculate mean, median, mode and bar chart based on the following table, where n_i denotes the absolute frequency of each value x_i:

x_i	n_i
22	8
30	2
38	6
46	3
54	4
62	9

128 Calculate mean, median, mode and bar chart based on the following table, where n_i denotes the absolute frequency of each value x_i:

x_i	n_i
35	7
40	9
45	5
50	3
55	6
60	1

129 Calculate mean, median, mode and bar chart based on the following table, where n_i denotes the absolute frequency of each value x_i:

x_i	n_i
25	5
33	8
41	2
49	9
57	7
65	4

130 Calculate mean, median, mode and bar chart based on the following table, where n_i denotes the absolute frequency of each value x_i:

x_i	n_i
~~32~~	~~5~~
39	9
46	7
53	6
60	3
67	8

131 Calculate mean, median, mode, standard deviation, mean absolute deviation, coefficient of variation, and bar chart based on the following table, where n_i denotes the absolute frequency of each value x_i:

x_i	n_i
22	1
24	6
26	7
28	2

132 Calculate mean, median, mode, standard deviation, mean absolute deviation, coefficient of variation, and bar chart based on the following table, where n_i denotes the absolute frequency of each value x_i:

x_i	n_i
19	7
21	3
23	8
25	5

133 Calculate mean, median, mode, standard deviation, mean absolute deviation, coefficient of variation, and bar chart based on the following table, where n_i denotes the absolute frequency of each value x_i:

x_i	n_i
0	1
9	5
18	8
27	9

23

134 Calculate mean, median, mode, standard deviation, mean absolute deviation, coefficient of variation, and bar chart based on the following table, where n_i denotes the absolute frequency of each value x_i:

x_i	n_i
13	5
22	6
31	4
40	3

135 Calculate mean, median, mode, standard deviation, mean absolute deviation, coefficient of variation, and bar chart based on the following table, where n_i denotes the absolute frequency of each value x_i:

x_i	n_i
0	7
9	2
18	5
27	4

136 Calculate mean, median, mode, standard deviation, mean absolute deviation, coefficient of variation, and bar chart based on the following table, where n_i denotes the absolute frequency of each value x_i:

x_i	n_i
0	5
5	4
10	7
15	2

137 Calculate mean, median, mode, standard deviation, mean absolute deviation, coefficient of variation, and bar chart based on the following table, where n_i denotes the absolute frequency of each value x_i:

x_i	n_i
13	6
16	7
19	2
22	5

138 Calculate mean, median, mode, standard deviation, mean absolute deviation, coefficient of variation, and bar chart based on the following table, where n_i denotes the absolute frequency of each value x_i:

x_i	n_i
20	3
~~24~~	~~1~~
28	5
32	4

139 Calculate mean, median, mode, standard deviation, mean absolute deviation, coefficient of variation, and bar chart based on the following table, where n_i denotes the absolute frequency of each value x_i:

x_i	n_i
27	4
~~36~~	~~9~~
45	6
54	3

140 Calculate mean, median, mode, standard deviation, mean absolute deviation, coefficient of variation, and bar chart based on the following table, where n_i denotes the absolute frequency of each value x_i:

x_i	n_i
16	5
~~18~~	~~4~~
20	3
22	2

141 Calculate mean, median, mode, standard deviation, mean absolute deviation, coefficient of variation, and bar chart based on the following table, where n_i denotes the absolute frequency of each value x_i:

x_i	n_i
10	4
~~13~~	~~3~~
16	6
19	5

142 Calculate mean, median, mode, standard deviation, mean absolute deviation, coefficient of variation, and bar chart based on the following table, where n_i denotes the absolute frequency of each value x_i:

x_i	n_i
4	8
6	9
8	7
10	5

143 Calculate mean, median, mode, standard deviation, mean absolute deviation, coefficient of variation, and bar chart based on the following table, where n_i denotes the absolute frequency of each value x_i:

x_i	n_i
14	6
18	3
22	5
26	1

144 Calculate mean, median, mode, standard deviation, mean absolute deviation, coefficient of variation, and bar chart based on the following table, where n_i denotes the absolute frequency of each value x_i:

x_i	n_i
9	2
12	8
15	6
18	1

145 Calculate mean, median, mode, standard deviation, mean absolute deviation, coefficient of variation, and bar chart based on the following table, where n_i denotes the absolute frequency of each value x_i:

x_i	n_i
0	6
3	2
6	4
9	5

146 Calculate mean, median, mode, standard deviation, mean absolute deviation, coefficient of variation, and bar chart based on the following table, where n_i denotes the absolute frequency of each value x_i:

x_i	n_i
24	3
27	2
30	6
33	4

147 Calculate mean, median, mode, standard deviation, mean absolute deviation, coefficient of variation, and bar chart based on the following table, where n_i denotes the absolute frequency of each value x_i:

x_i	n_i
22	3
27	5
32	9
37	8

148 Calculate mean, median, mode, standard deviation, mean absolute deviation, coefficient of variation, and bar chart based on the following table, where n_i denotes the absolute frequency of each value x_i:

x_i	n_i
18	8
25	6
32	1
39	4

149 Calculate mean, median, mode, standard deviation, mean absolute deviation, coefficient of variation, and bar chart based on the following table, where n_i denotes the absolute frequency of each value x_i:

x_i	n_i
30	9
38	3
46	1
54	7

150 Calculate mean, median, mode, standard deviation, mean absolute deviation, coefficient of variation, and bar chart based on the following table, where n_i denotes the absolute frequency of each value x_i:

x_i	n_i
0	9
7	4
14	2
21	6

151 Calculate mean, median, mode, standard deviation, mean absolute deviation, coefficient of variation, and bar chart based on the following table, where n_i denotes the absolute frequency of each value x_i:

x_i	n_i
8	8
14	5
20	3
26	7

152 Calculate mean, median, mode, standard deviation, mean absolute deviation, coefficient of variation, and bar chart based on the following table, where n_i denotes the absolute frequency of each value x_i:

x_i	n_i
0	2
6	6
12	7
18	5

153 Calculate mean, median, mode, standard deviation, mean absolute deviation, coefficient of variation, and bar chart based on the following table, where n_i denotes the absolute frequency of each value x_i:

x_i	n_i
24	2
33	9
42	3
51	8

154 Calculate mean, median, mode, standard deviation, mean absolute deviation, coefficient of variation, and bar chart based on the following table, where n_i denotes the absolute frequency of each value x_i:

x_i	n_i
27	2
34	6
41	4
48	8

155 Calculate mean, median, mode, standard deviation, mean absolute deviation, coefficient of variation, and bar chart based on the following table, where n_i denotes the absolute frequency of each value x_i:

x_i	n_i
8	2
14	8
20	4
26	1

156 Calculate mean, median, mode, standard deviation, mean absolute deviation, coefficient of variation, and bar chart based on the following table, where n_i denotes the absolute frequency of each value x_i:

x_i	n_i
0	7
2	4
4	6
6	3

157 Calculate mean, median, mode, standard deviation, mean absolute deviation, coefficient of variation, and bar chart based on the following table, where n_i denotes the absolute frequency of each value x_i:

x_i	n_i
7	2
12	4
17	8
22	6

158 Calculate mean, median, mode, standard deviation, mean absolute deviation, coefficient of variation, and bar chart based on the following table, where n_i denotes the absolute frequency of each value x_i:

x_i	n_i
0	4
4	7
8	9
12	1

159 Calculate mean, median, mode, standard deviation, mean absolute deviation, coefficient of variation, and bar chart based on the following table, where n_i denotes the absolute frequency of each value x_i:

x_i	n_i
0	6
3	2
6	5
9	3

160 Calculate mean, median, mode, standard deviation, mean absolute deviation, coefficient of variation, and bar chart based on the following table, where n_i denotes the absolute frequency of each value x_i:

x_i	n_i
21	9
24	3
27	6
30	4

161 Calculate mean, median, mode, standard deviation, mean absolute deviation, coefficient of variation, and bar chart based on the following table, where n_i denotes the absolute frequency of each value x_i:

x_i	n_i
9	7
13	6
17	9
21	3

162 Calculate mean, median, mode, standard deviation, mean absolute deviation, coefficient of variation, and bar chart based on the following table, where n_i denotes the absolute frequency of each value x_i:

x_i	n_i
27	8
35	7
43	2
51	6

163 Calculate mean, median, mode, standard deviation, mean absolute deviation, coefficient of variation, and bar chart based on the following table, where n_i denotes the absolute frequency of each value x_i:

x_i	n_i
0	2
6	9
12	4
18	5

164 Calculate mean, median, mode, standard deviation, mean absolute deviation, coefficient of variation, and bar chart based on the following table, where n_i denotes the absolute frequency of each value x_i:

x_i	n_i
0	3
2	9
4	7
6	5
8	8

165 Calculate mean, median, mode, standard deviation, mean absolute deviation, coefficient of variation, and bar chart based on the following table, where n_i denotes the absolute frequency of each value x_i:

x_i	n_i
0	4
2	1
4	7
6	2
8	5

166 Calculate mean, median, mode, standard deviation, mean absolute deviation, coefficient of variation, and bar chart based on the following table, where n_i denotes the absolute frequency of each value x_i:

x_i	n_i
0	5
8	6
16	7
24	3
32	8

167 Calculate mean, median, mode, standard deviation, mean absolute deviation, coefficient of variation, and bar chart based on the following table, where n_i denotes the absolute frequency of each value x_i:

x_i	n_i
0	8
10	5
20	4
30	6
40	7

168 Calculate mean, median, mode, standard deviation, mean absolute deviation, coefficient of variation, and bar chart based on the following table, where n_i denotes the absolute frequency of each value x_i:

x_i	n_i
32	8
37	3
42	4
47	1
52	7

169 Calculate mean, median, mode, standard deviation, mean absolute deviation, coefficient of variation, and bar chart based on the following table, where n_i denotes the absolute frequency of each value x_i:

x_i	n_i
22	7
24	3
26	9
28	8
30	6

170 Calculate mean, median, mode, standard deviation, mean absolute deviation, coefficient of variation, and bar chart based on the following table, where n_i denotes the absolute frequency of each value x_i:

x_i	n_i
0	2
6	5
12	3
18	7
24	9

171 Calculate mean, median, mode, standard deviation, mean absolute deviation, coefficient of variation, and bar chart based on the following table, where n_i denotes the absolute frequency of each value x_i:

x_i	n_i
35	3
40	4
45	7
50	8
55	5

172 Calculate mean, median, mode, standard deviation, mean absolute deviation, coefficient of variation, and bar chart based on the following table, where n_i denotes the absolute frequency of each value x_i:

x_i	n_i
17	8
25	1
33	6
41	5
49	4

173 Calculate mean, median, mode, standard deviation, mean absolute deviation, coefficient of variation, and bar chart based on the following table, where n_i denotes the absolute frequency of each value x_i:

x_i	n_i
25	5
34	8
43	7
52	6
61	2

174 Calculate mean, median, mode, standard deviation, mean absolute deviation, coefficient of variation, and bar chart based on the following table, where n_i denotes the absolute frequency of each value x_i:

x_i	n_i
27	4
32	9
37	5
42	1
47	2

175 Calculate mean, median, mode, standard deviation, mean absolute deviation, coefficient of variation, and bar chart based on the following table, where n_i denotes the absolute frequency of each value x_i:

x_i	n_i
36	7
43	4
50	3
57	6
64	1

176 Calculate mean, median, mode, standard deviation, mean absolute deviation, coefficient of variation, and bar chart based on the following table, where n_i denotes the absolute frequency of each value x_i:

x_i	n_i
0	9
8	7
16	2
24	3
32	6

177 Calculate mean, median, mode, standard deviation, mean absolute deviation, coefficient of variation, and bar chart based on the following table, where n_i denotes the absolute frequency of each value x_i:

x_i	n_i
20	3
28	8
36	6
44	5
52	7

178 Calculate mean, median, mode, standard deviation, mean absolute deviation, coefficient of variation, and bar chart based on the following table, where n_i denotes the absolute frequency of each value x_i:

x_i	n_i
25	2
27	6
29	3
31	9
33	8

179 Calculate mean, median, mode, standard deviation, mean absolute deviation, coefficient of variation, and bar chart based on the following table, where n_i denotes the absolute frequency of each value x_i:

x_i	n_i
12	5
16	2
20	3
24	9
28	6

180 Calculate mean, median, mode, standard deviation, mean absolute deviation, coefficient of variation, and bar chart based on the following table, where n_i denotes the absolute frequency of each value x_i:

x_i	n_i
11	7
14	1
17	2
20	3
23	4

181 Calculate mean, median, mode, standard deviation, mean absolute deviation, coefficient of variation, and bar chart based on the following table, where n_i denotes the absolute frequency of each value x_i:

x_i	n_i
22	8
26	6
30	5
34	2
38	3

182 Calculate mean, median, mode, standard deviation, mean absolute deviation, coefficient of variation, and bar chart based on the following table, where n_i denotes the absolute frequency of each value x_i:

x_i	n_i
30	3
39	5
48	9
57	4
66	7

183 Calculate mean, median, mode, standard deviation, mean absolute deviation, coefficient of variation, and bar chart based on the following table, where n_i denotes the absolute frequency of each value x_i:

x_i	n_i
9	1
16	3
23	5
30	6
37	7

184 Calculate mean, median, mode, standard deviation, mean absolute deviation, coefficient of variation, and bar chart based on the following table, where n_i denotes the absolute frequency of each value x_i:

x_i	n_i
24	8
29	7
34	4
39	5
44	9

185 Calculate mean, median, mode, standard deviation, mean absolute deviation, coefficient of variation, and bar chart based on the following table, where n_i denotes the absolute frequency of each value x_i:

x_i	n_i
28	2
34	7
40	9
46	6
52	3

186 Calculate mean, median, mode, standard deviation, mean absolute deviation, coefficient of variation, and bar chart based on the following table, where n_i denotes the absolute frequency of each value x_i:

x_i	n_i
24	7
~~32~~	~~2~~
40	4
48	8
56	3

187 Calculate mean, median, mode, standard deviation, mean absolute deviation, coefficient of variation, and bar chart based on the following table, where n_i denotes the absolute frequency of each value x_i:

x_i	n_i
0	3
5	7
10	4
15	9
20	2

188 Calculate mean, median, mode, standard deviation, mean absolute deviation, coefficient of variation, and bar chart based on the following table, where n_i denotes the absolute frequency of each value x_i:

x_i	n_i
13	6
20	2
27	7
34	1
41	3

189 Calculate mean, median, mode, standard deviation, mean absolute deviation, coefficient of variation, and bar chart based on the following table, where n_i denotes the absolute frequency of each value x_i:

x_i	n_i
25	3
26	5
27	7
28	8
29	6

190 Calculate mean, median, mode, standard deviation, mean absolute deviation, coefficient of variation, and bar chart based on the following table, where n_i denotes the absolute frequency of each value x_i:

x_i	n_i
0	3
1	4
2	7
3	5
4	2

191 Calculate mean, median, mode, standard deviation, mean absolute deviation, coefficient of variation, and bar chart based on the following table, where n_i denotes the absolute frequency of each value x_i:

x_i	n_i
13	6
21	2
29	8
37	5
45	7

192 Calculate mean, median, mode, standard deviation, mean absolute deviation, coefficient of variation, and bar chart based on the following table, where n_i denotes the absolute frequency of each value x_i:

x_i	n_i
32	3
34	7
36	5
38	2
40	9

193 Calculate mean, median, mode, standard deviation, mean absolute deviation, coefficient of variation, and bar chart based on the following table, where n_i denotes the absolute frequency of each value x_i:

x_i	n_i
33	8
39	4
45	3
51	6
57	2

194 Calculate mean, median, mode, standard deviation, mean absolute deviation, coefficient of variation, and bar chart based on the following table, where n_i denotes the absolute frequency of each value x_i:

x_i	n_i
29	4
35	1
41	8
47	7
53	6

195 Calculate mean, median, mode, standard deviation, mean absolute deviation, coefficient of variation, and bar chart based on the following table, where n_i denotes the absolute frequency of each value x_i:

x_i	n_i
5	2
8	7
11	6
14	4
17	1

196 Calculate mean, median, mode, standard deviation, mean absolute deviation, coefficient of variation, and bar chart based on the following table, where n_i denotes the absolute frequency of each value x_i:

x_i	n_i
31	7
34	4
37	2
40	3
43	5

197 Calculate mean, median, mode, standard deviation, mean absolute deviation, coefficient of variation, and bar chart based on the following table, where n_i denotes the absolute frequency of each value x_i:

x_i	n_i
15	7
23	1
31	2
39	8
47	5

198 Calculate mean, median, mode, standard deviation, mean absolute deviation, coefficient of variation, and bar chart based on the following table, where n_i denotes the absolute frequency of each value x_i:

x_i	n_i
22	7
24	3
26	5
28	9
30	8
32	2

199 Calculate mean, median, mode, standard deviation, mean absolute deviation, coefficient of variation, and bar chart based on the following table, where n_i denotes the absolute frequency of each value x_i:

x_i	n_i
30	5
36	3
42	2
48	9
54	6
60	7

200 Calculate mean, median, mode, standard deviation, mean absolute deviation, coefficient of variation, and bar chart based on the following table, where n_i denotes the absolute frequency of each value x_i:

x_i	n_i
26	5
27	4
28	7
29	3
30	6
31	9

201 Calculate mean, median, mode, standard deviation, mean absolute deviation, coefficient of variation, and bar chart based on the following table, where n_i denotes the absolute frequency of each value x_i:

x_i	n_i
31	6
34	5
37	4
40	7
43	8
46	9

202 Calculate mean, median, mode, standard deviation, mean absolute deviation, coefficient of variation, and bar chart based on the following table, where n_i denotes the absolute frequency of each value x_i:

x_i	n_i
25	1
30	6
35	8
40	7
45	2
50	4

203 Calculate mean, median, mode, standard deviation, mean absolute deviation, coefficient of variation, and bar chart based on the following table, where n_i denotes the absolute frequency of each value x_i:

x_i	n_i
0	8
4	3
8	2
12	4
16	5
20	9

204 Calculate mean, median, mode, standard deviation, mean absolute deviation, coefficient of variation, and bar chart based on the following table, where n_i denotes the absolute frequency of each value x_i:

x_i	n_i
33	8
39	4
45	3
51	9
57	5
63	7

205 Calculate mean, median, mode, standard deviation, mean absolute deviation, coefficient of variation, and bar chart based on the following table, where n_i denotes the absolute frequency of each value x_i:

x_i	n_i
16	9
24	6
32	7
40	5
48	4
56	3

206 Calculate mean, median, mode, standard deviation, mean absolute deviation, coefficient of variation, and bar chart based on the following table, where n_i denotes the absolute frequency of each value x_i:

x_i	n_i
19	9
22	2
25	7
28	8
31	3
34	5

207 Calculate mean, median, mode, standard deviation, mean absolute deviation, coefficient of variation, and bar chart based on the following table, where n_i denotes the absolute frequency of each value x_i:

x_i	n_i
25	3
30	5
35	4
40	6
45	7
50	1

208 Calculate mean, median, mode, standard deviation, mean absolute deviation, coefficient of variation, and bar chart based on the following table, where n_i denotes the absolute frequency of each value x_i:

x_i	n_i
18	3
23	9
28	4
33	5
38	7
43	8

209 Calculate mean, median, mode, standard deviation, mean absolute deviation, coefficient of variation, and bar chart based on the following table, where n_i denotes the absolute frequency of each value x_i:

x_i	n_i
0	7
5	4
10	8
15	2
20	1
25	3

210 Calculate mean, median, mode, standard deviation, mean absolute deviation, coefficient of variation, and bar chart based on the following table, where n_i denotes the absolute frequency of each value x_i:

x_i	n_i
23	8
31	6
39	2
47	4
55	9
63	3

211 Calculate mean, median, mode, standard deviation, mean absolute deviation, coefficient of variation, and bar chart based on the following table, where n_i denotes the absolute frequency of each value x_i:

x_i	n_i
0	3
7	8
14	2
21	5
28	1
35	4

212 Calculate mean, median, mode, standard deviation, mean absolute deviation, coefficient of variation, and bar chart based on the following table, where n_i denotes the absolute frequency of each value x_i:

x_i	n_i
32	2
40	6
48	3
56	9
64	8
72	5

213 Calculate mean, median, mode, standard deviation, mean absolute deviation, coefficient of variation, and bar chart based on the following table, where n_i denotes the absolute frequency of each value x_i:

x_i	n_i
0	2
9	7
18	4
27	8
36	5
45	3

214 Calculate mean, median, mode, standard deviation, mean absolute deviation, coefficient of variation, and bar chart based on the following table, where n_i denotes the absolute frequency of each value x_i:

x_i	n_i
4	2
7	3
10	8
13	4
16	1
19	6

215 Calculate mean, median, mode, standard deviation, mean absolute deviation, coefficient of variation, and bar chart based on the following table, where n_i denotes the absolute frequency of each value x_i:

x_i	n_i
23	3
24	6
25	4
26	1
27	8
28	5

216 Calculate mean, median, mode, standard deviation, mean absolute deviation, coefficient of variation, and bar chart based on the following table, where n_i denotes the absolute frequency of each value x_i:

x_i	n_i
38	7
46	5
54	2
62	6
70	8
78	4

217 Calculate mean, median, mode, standard deviation, mean absolute deviation, coefficient of variation, and bar chart based on the following table, where n_i denotes the absolute frequency of each value x_i:

x_i	n_i
0	3
10	5
20	4
30	8
40	6
50	7

218 Calculate mean, median, mode, standard deviation, mean absolute deviation, coefficient of variation, and bar chart based on the following table, where n_i denotes the absolute frequency of each value x_i:

x_i	n_i
25	9
34	5
43	6
52	3
61	8
70	7

219 Calculate mean, median, mode, standard deviation, mean absolute deviation, coefficient of variation, and bar chart based on the following table, where n_i denotes the absolute frequency of each value x_i:

x_i	n_i
21	3
22	5
23	8
24	2
25	7
26	6

220 Calculate mean, median, mode, standard deviation, mean absolute deviation, coefficient of variation, and bar chart based on the following table, where n_i denotes the absolute frequency of each value x_i:

x_i	n_i
30	3
32	6
34	2
36	4
38	9
40	7

221 Calculate mean, median, mode, standard deviation, mean absolute deviation, coefficient of variation, and bar chart based on the following table, where n_i denotes the absolute frequency of each value x_i:

x_i	n_i
30	6
34	8
38	5
42	2
46	4
50	3

222 Calculate mean, median, mode, standard deviation, mean absolute deviation, coefficient of variation, and bar chart based on the following table, where n_i denotes the absolute frequency of each value x_i:

x_i	n_i
23	9
26	6
29	2
32	4
35	7
38	5

223 Calculate mean, median, mode, standard deviation, mean absolute deviation, coefficient of variation, and bar chart based on the following table, where n_i denotes the absolute frequency of each value x_i:

x_i	n_i
7	4
11	2
15	5
19	3
23	9
27	7

224 Calculate mean, median, mode, standard deviation, mean absolute deviation, coefficient of variation, and bar chart based on the following table, where n_i denotes the absolute frequency of each value x_i:

x_i	n_i
19	1
23	5
27	3
31	8
35	9
39	7

225 Calculate mean, median, mode, standard deviation, mean absolute deviation, coefficient of variation, and bar chart based on the following table, where n_i denotes the absolute frequency of each value x_i:

x_i	n_i
17	1
20	9
23	6
26	7
29	4
32	2

226 Calculate mean, median, mode, standard deviation, mean absolute deviation, coefficient of variation, and bar chart based on the following table, where n_i denotes the absolute frequency of each value x_i:

x_i	n_i
35	4
41	1
47	3
53	5
59	2
65	8

227 Calculate mean, median, mode, standard deviation, mean absolute deviation, coefficient of variation, and bar chart based on the following table, where n_i denotes the absolute frequency of each value x_i:

x_i	n_i
0	9
6	3
12	4
18	6
24	2
30	5

228 Calculate mean, median, mode, standard deviation, mean absolute deviation, coefficient of variation, and bar chart based on the following table, where n_i denotes the absolute frequency of each value x_i:

x_i	n_i
0	4
8	8
16	5
24	2
32	6
40	9

229 Calculate mean, median, mode, standard deviation, mean absolute deviation, coefficient of variation, and bar chart based on the following table, where n_i denotes the absolute frequency of each value x_i:

x_i	n_i
8	7
14	8
20	3
26	2
32	4
38	5

Solutions

1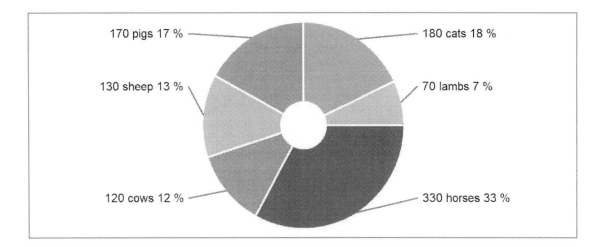

2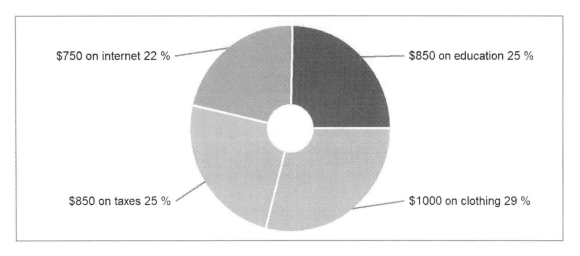

3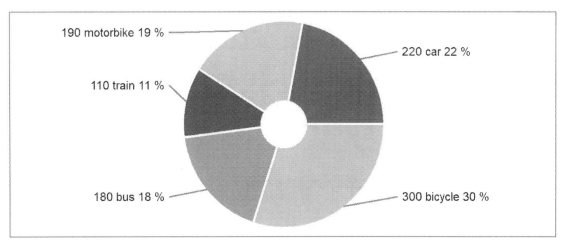

4

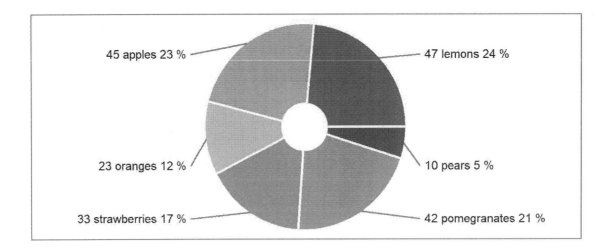

45 apples 23 %

47 lemons 24 %

10 pears 5 %

23 oranges 12 %

42 pomegranates 21 %

33 strawberries 17 %

5

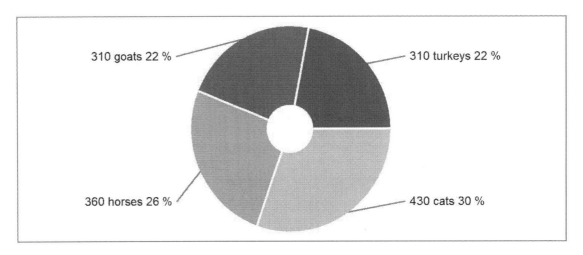

310 goats 22 %

310 turkeys 22 %

360 horses 26 %

430 cats 30 %

6

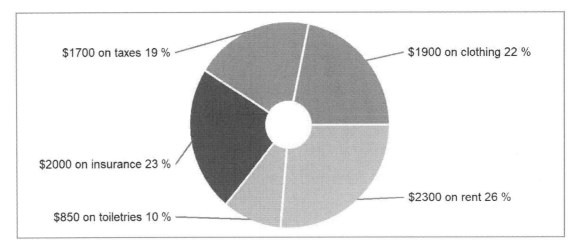

$1700 on taxes 19 %

$1900 on clothing 22 %

$2000 on insurance 23 %

$2300 on rent 26 %

$850 on toiletries 10 %

7

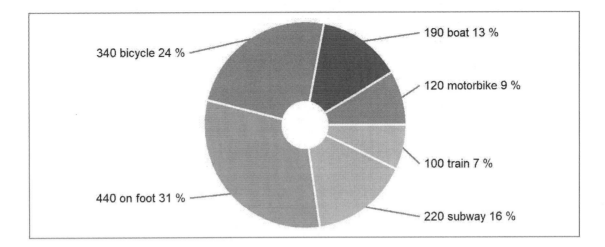

340 bicycle 24 %

190 boat 13 %

120 motorbike 9 %

100 train 7 %

220 subway 16 %

440 on foot 31 %

8

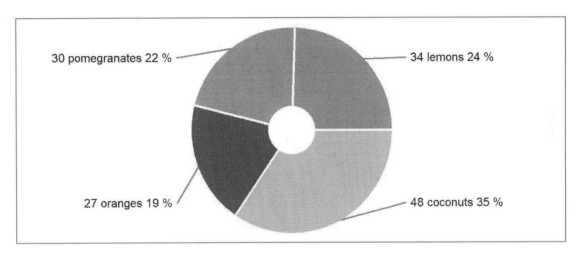

30 pomegranates 22 %

34 lemons 24 %

27 oranges 19 %

48 coconuts 35 %

9

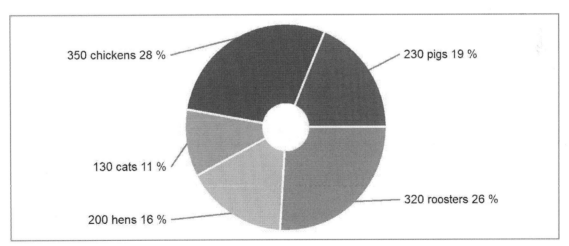

350 chickens 28 %

230 pigs 19 %

130 cats 11 %

320 roosters 26 %

200 hens 16 %

10

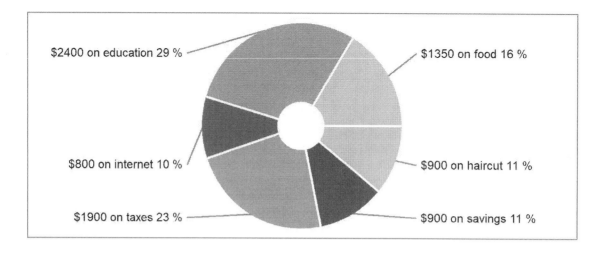

$2400 on education 29 %

$1350 on food 16 %

$800 on internet 10 %

$900 on haircut 11 %

$1900 on taxes 23 %

$900 on savings 11 %

11

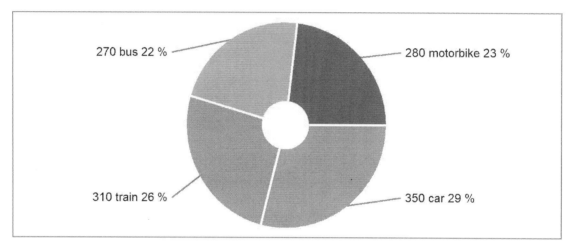

270 bus 22 %

280 motorbike 23 %

310 train 26 %

350 car 29 %

12

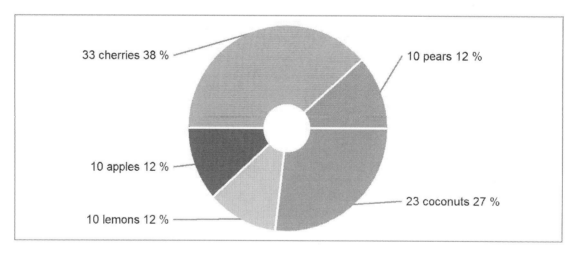

33 cherries 38 %

10 pears 12 %

10 apples 12 %

23 coconuts 27 %

10 lemons 12 %

13

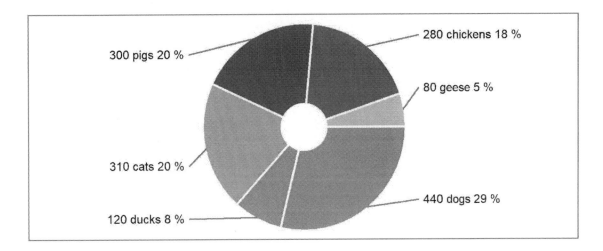

14

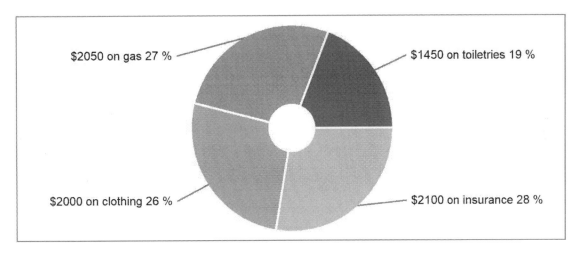

15

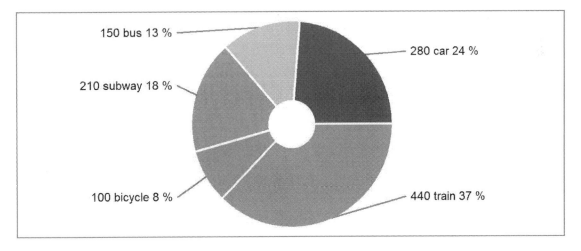

16

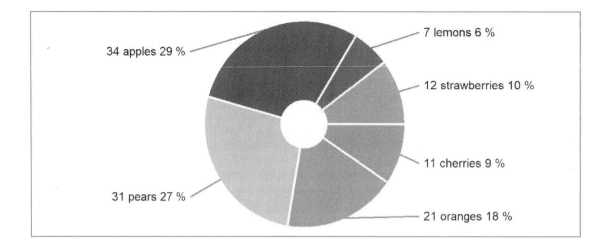

17

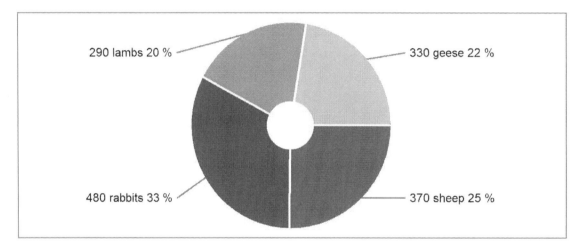

18

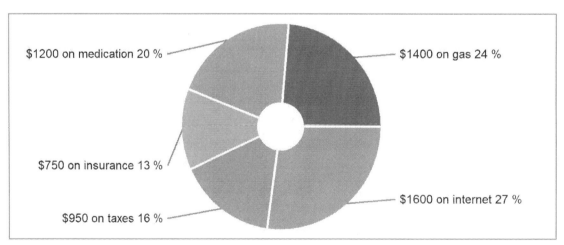

19

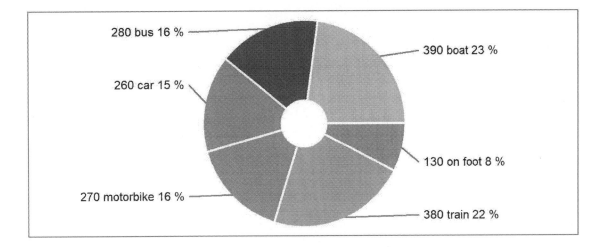

280 bus 16 %
390 boat 23 %
260 car 15 %
130 on foot 8 %
270 motorbike 16 %
380 train 22 %

20

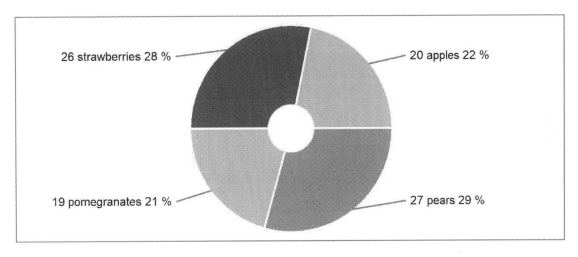

26 strawberries 28 %
20 apples 22 %
19 pomegranates 21 %
27 pears 29 %

21

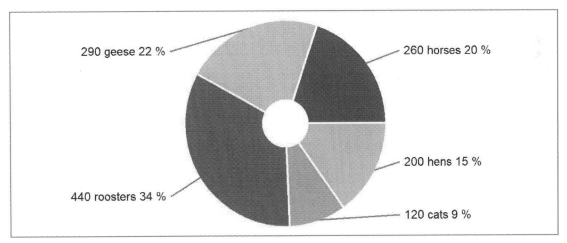

290 geese 22 %
260 horses 20 %
200 hens 15 %
440 roosters 34 %
120 cats 9 %

22

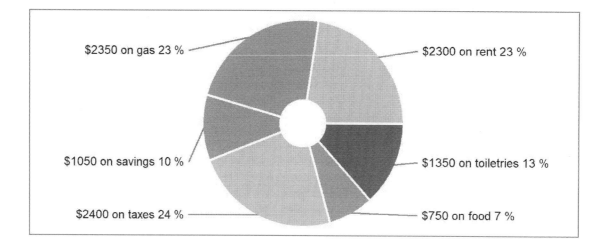

$2350 on gas 23 %

$2300 on rent 23 %

$1050 on savings 10 %

$1350 on toiletries 13 %

$2400 on taxes 24 %

$750 on food 7 %

23

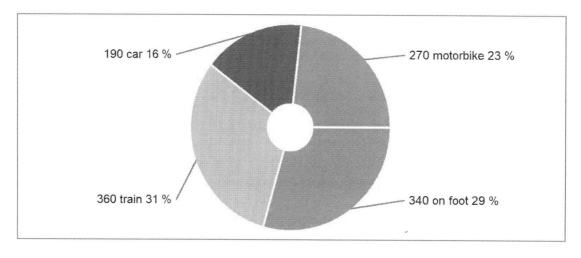

190 car 16 %

270 motorbike 23 %

360 train 31 %

340 on foot 29 %

24

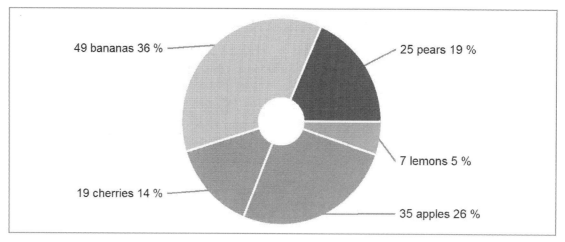

49 bananas 36 %

25 pears 19 %

7 lemons 5 %

19 cherries 14 %

35 apples 26 %

25

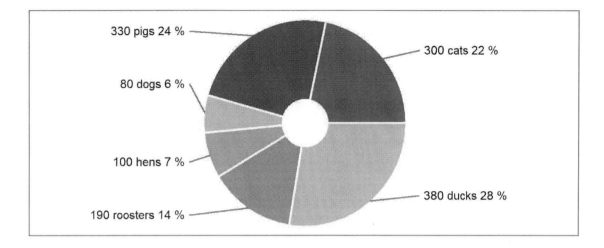

330 pigs 24 %

300 cats 22 %

80 dogs 6 %

100 hens 7 %

190 roosters 14 %

380 ducks 28 %

26

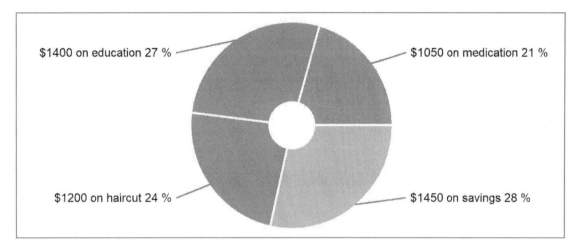

$1400 on education 27 %

$1050 on medication 21 %

$1200 on haircut 24 %

$1450 on savings 28 %

27

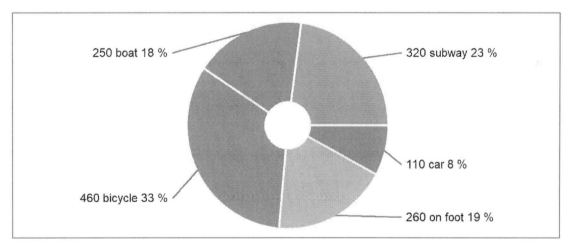

250 boat 18 %

320 subway 23 %

460 bicycle 33 %

110 car 8 %

260 on foot 19 %

28

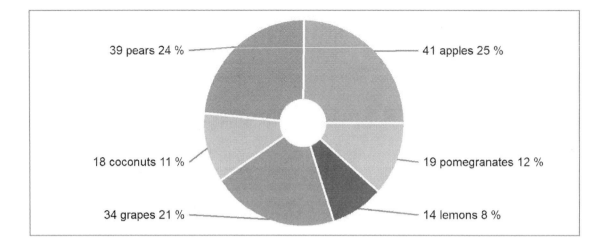

29

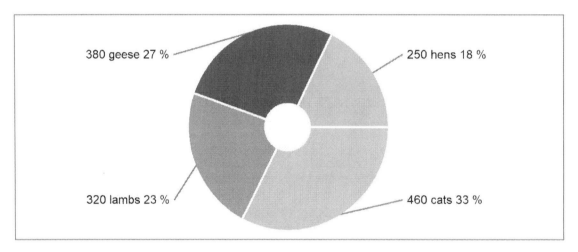

30

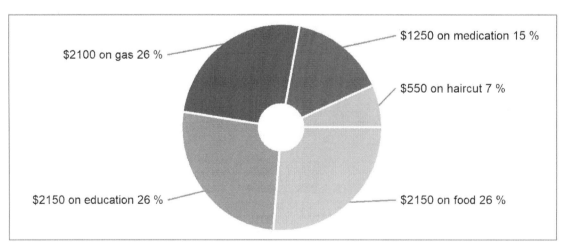

31

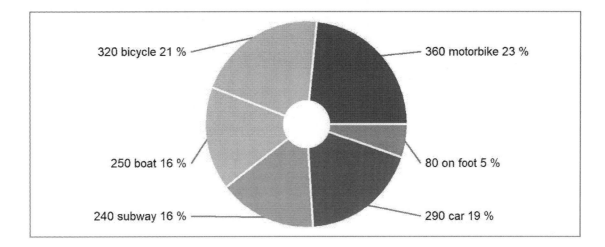

320 bicycle 21 %

360 motorbike 23 %

250 boat 16 %

80 on foot 5 %

240 subway 16 %

290 car 19 %

32

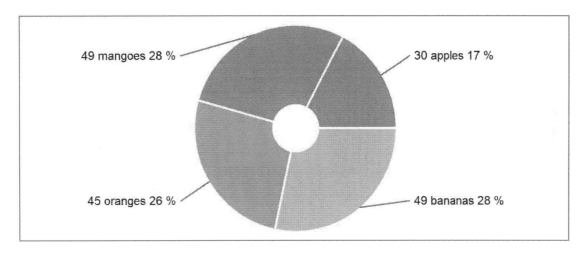

49 mangoes 28 %

30 apples 17 %

45 oranges 26 %

49 bananas 28 %

33

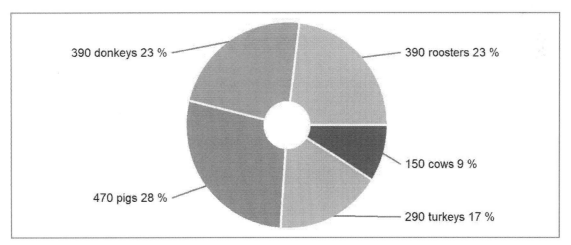

390 donkeys 23 %

390 roosters 23 %

150 cows 9 %

470 pigs 28 %

290 turkeys 17 %

34

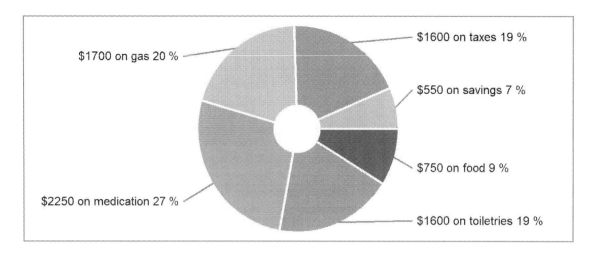

35

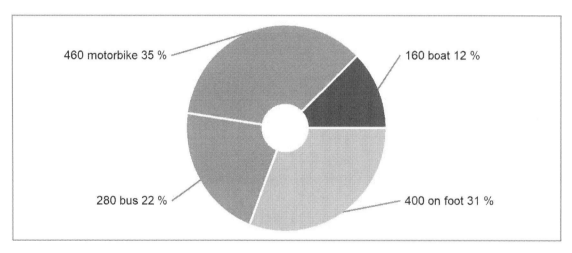

36

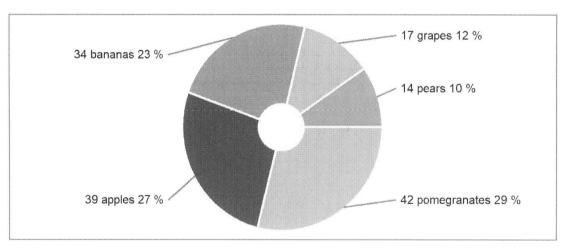

37

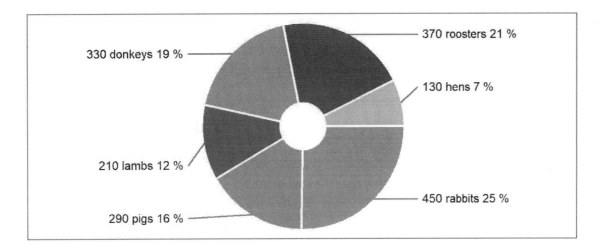

330 donkeys 19 %

370 roosters 21 %

130 hens 7 %

210 lambs 12 %

450 rabbits 25 %

290 pigs 16 %

38

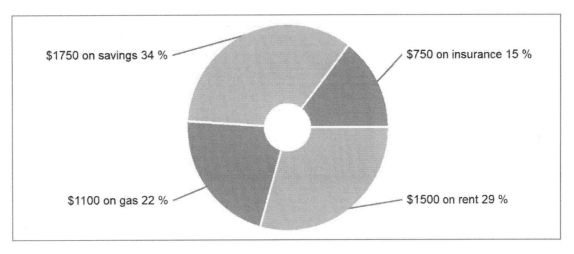

$1750 on savings 34 %

$750 on insurance 15 %

$1100 on gas 22 %

$1500 on rent 29 %

39

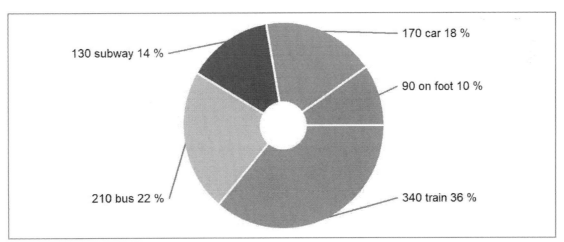

130 subway 14 %

170 car 18 %

90 on foot 10 %

210 bus 22 %

340 train 36 %

40

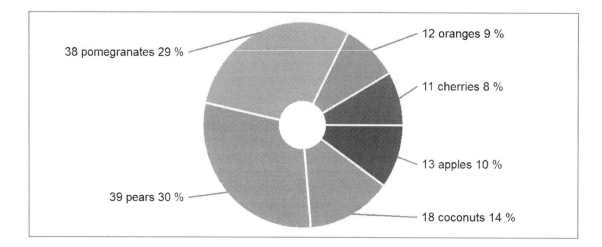

38 pomegranates 29 %
12 oranges 9 %
11 cherries 8 %
13 apples 10 %
18 coconuts 14 %
39 pears 30 %

41

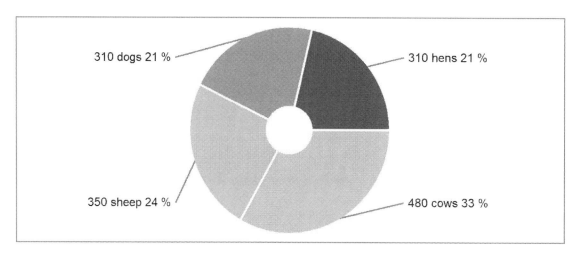

310 dogs 21 %
310 hens 21 %
350 sheep 24 %
480 cows 33 %

42

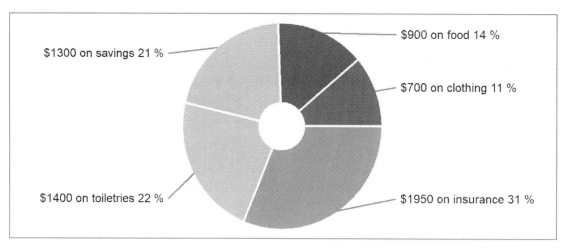

$1300 on savings 21 %
$900 on food 14 %
$700 on clothing 11 %
$1400 on toiletries 22 %
$1950 on insurance 31 %

43

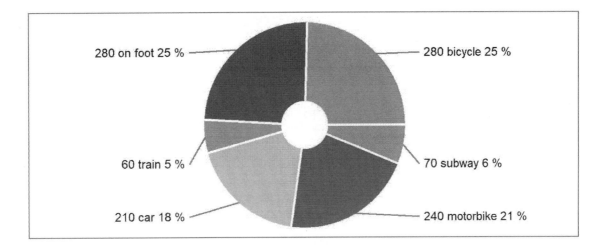

280 on foot 25 %

280 bicycle 25 %

60 train 5 %

70 subway 6 %

210 car 18 %

240 motorbike 21 %

44

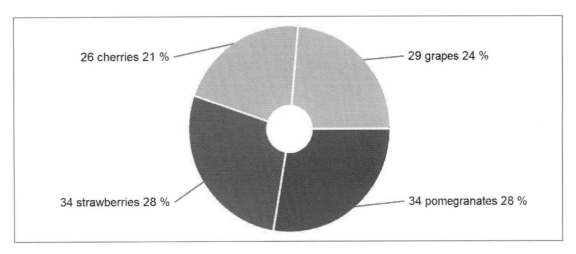

26 cherries 21 %

29 grapes 24 %

34 strawberries 28 %

34 pomegranates 28 %

45

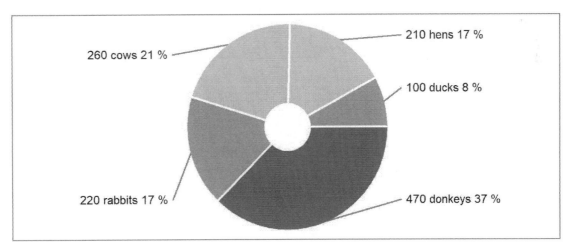

260 cows 21 %

210 hens 17 %

100 ducks 8 %

220 rabbits 17 %

470 donkeys 37 %

46

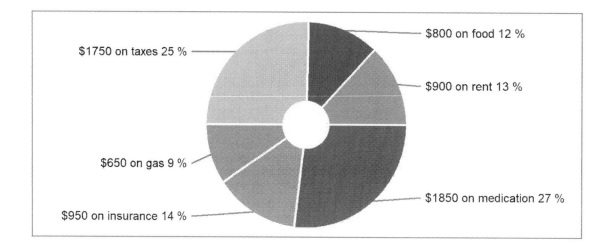

$1750 on taxes 25 %
$800 on food 12 %
$900 on rent 13 %
$650 on gas 9 %
$1850 on medication 27 %
$950 on insurance 14 %

47

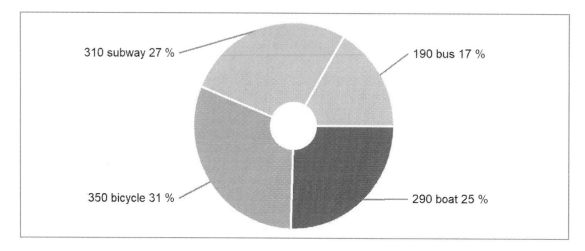

310 subway 27 %
190 bus 17 %
350 bicycle 31 %
290 boat 25 %

48

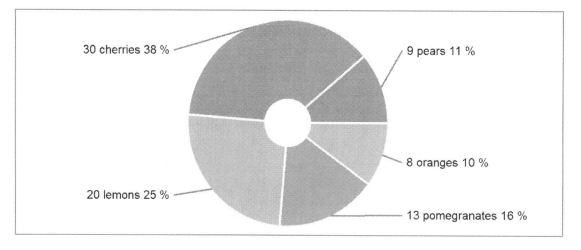

30 cherries 38 %
9 pears 11 %
8 oranges 10 %
20 lemons 25 %
13 pomegranates 16 %

49

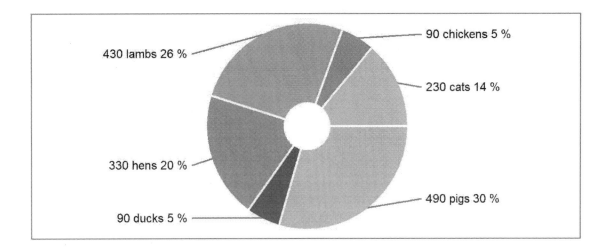

50

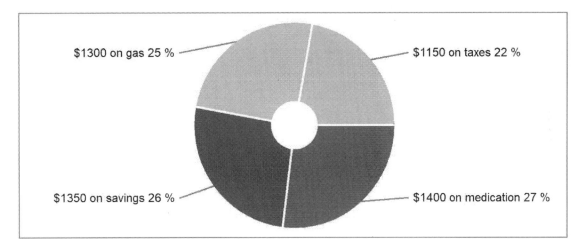

51

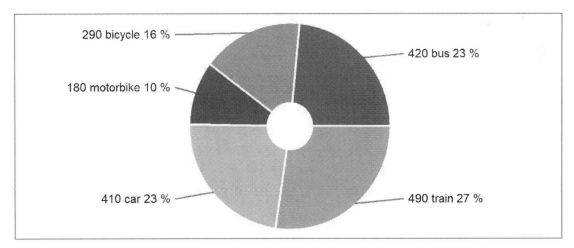

52

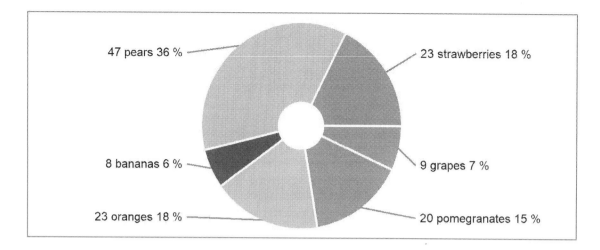

53

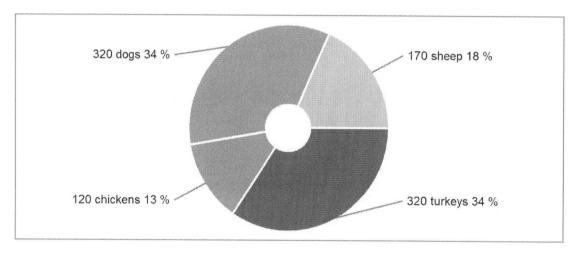

54

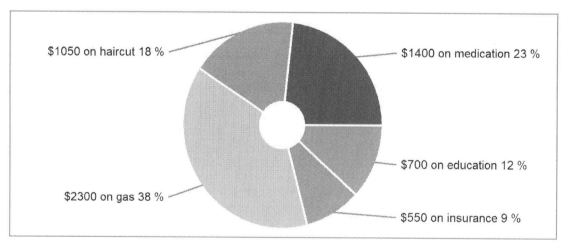

55

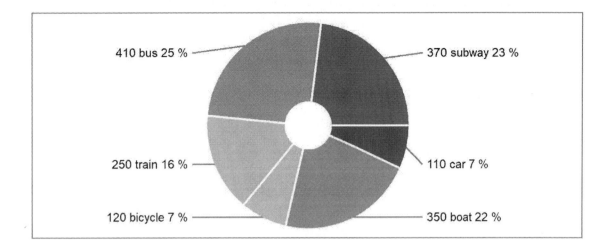

56

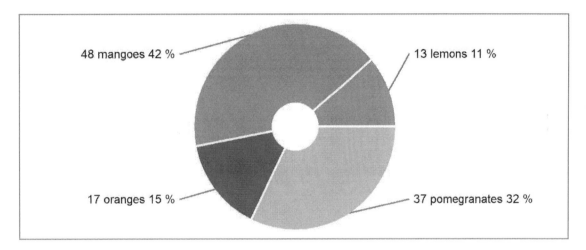

57

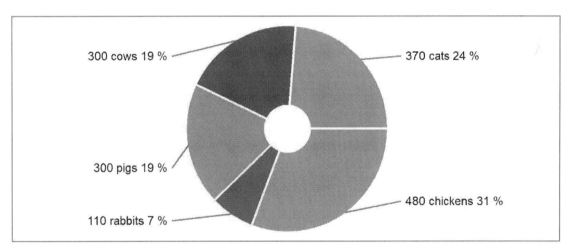

58

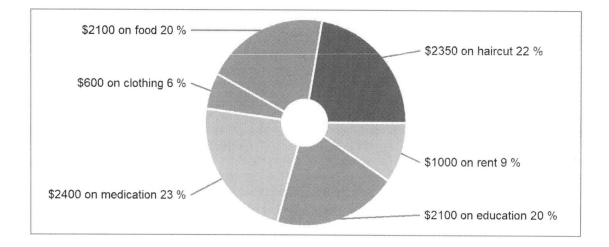

59

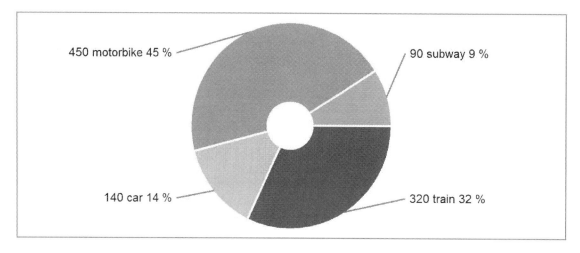

60

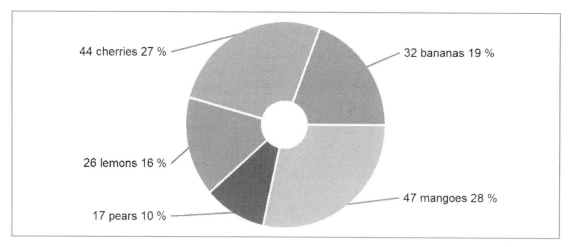

61

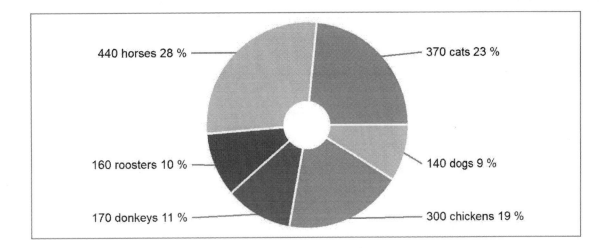

440 horses 28 %
370 cats 23 %
160 roosters 10 %
140 dogs 9 %
170 donkeys 11 %
300 chickens 19 %

62

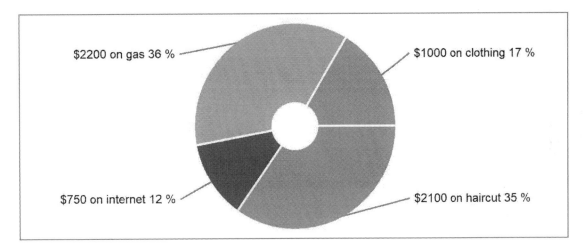

$2200 on gas 36 %
$1000 on clothing 17 %
$750 on internet 12 %
$2100 on haircut 35 %

63

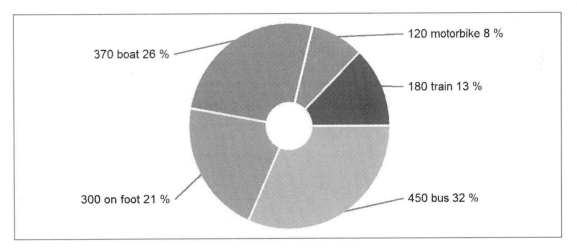

370 boat 26 %
120 motorbike 8 %
180 train 13 %
300 on foot 21 %
450 bus 32 %

64

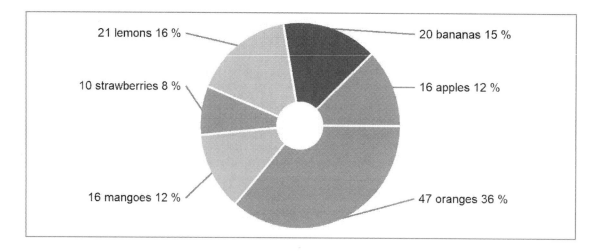

65

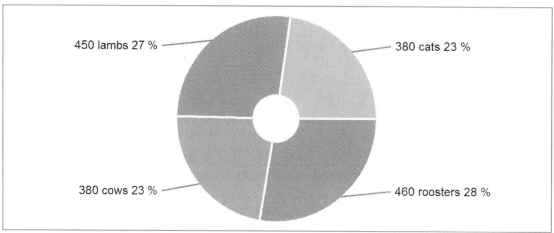

66 $\overline{x} = 23.714$ $Me = 26$ $Mo = 34$

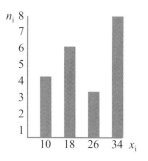

67 $\overline{x} = 30.091$ $Me = 29$ $Mo = 25$

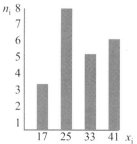

68 $\bar{x} = 16.9$ $Me = 16$ $Mo = 19$

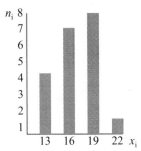

69 $\bar{x} = 6.933$ $Me = 8$ $Mo = 8$

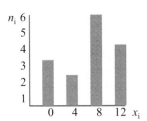

70 $\bar{x} = 12.842$ $Me = 12$ $Mo = 16$

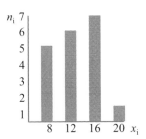

71 $\bar{x} = 5.778$ $Me = 4$ $Mo = 4$

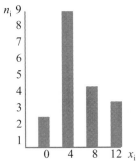

72 $\bar{x} = 29.9$ $Me = 26$ $Mo = 38$

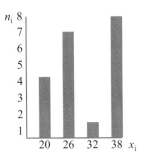

73 $\overline{x} = 8.8$ $Me = 8$ $Mo = 0$

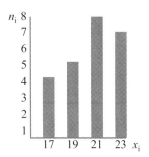

74 $\overline{x} = 20.5$ $Me = 21$ $Mo = 21$

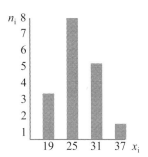

75 $\overline{x} = 26.412$ $Me = 25$ $Mo = 25$

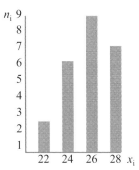

76 $\overline{x} = 25.75$ $Me = 26$ $Mo = 26$

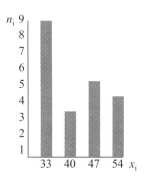

77 $\overline{x} = 41.333$ $Me = 40$ $Mo = 33$

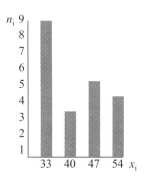

78 $\overline{x} = 15.294$ $Me = 10$ $Mo = 30$

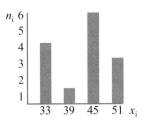

79 $\overline{x} = 42.429$ $Me = 45$ $Mo = 45$

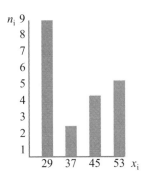

80 $\overline{x} = 39$ $Me = 37$ $Mo = 29$

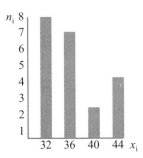

81 $\overline{x} = 36.381$ $Me = 36$ $Mo = 32$

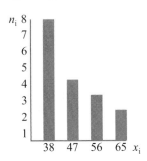

82 $\overline{x} = 46.471$ $Me = 47$ $Mo = 38$

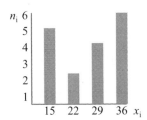

83 $\overline{x} = 26.529$ $Me = 29$ $Mo = 36$

84 $\overline{x} = 14.111$ $Me = 14$ $Mo = 12$

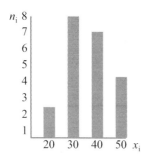

85 $\overline{x} = 36.19$ $Me = 40$ $Mo = 30$

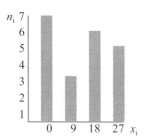

86 $\overline{x} = 12.857$ $Me = 18$ $Mo = 0$

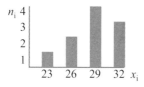

87 $\overline{x} = 28.7$ $Me = 29$ $Mo = 29$

88 $\overline{x} = 42.583$ $Me = 38$ $Mo = 33$

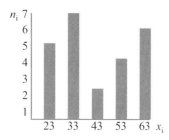

89 $\overline{x} = 57.4$ $Me = 61$ $Mo = 61$

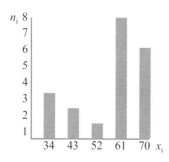

90 $\bar{x} = 27$ $Me = 27$ $Mo = 32$

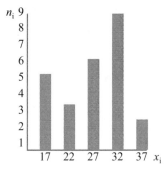

91 $\bar{x} = 22.958$ $Me = 22.5$ $Mo = 22$

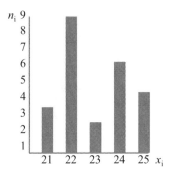

92 $\bar{x} = 26.529$ $Me = 27$ $Mo = 35$

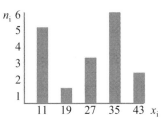

93 $\bar{x} = 11$ $Me = 12$ $Mo = 0$

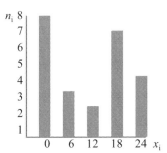

94 $\bar{x} = 26.8$ $Me = 24$ $Mo = 24$

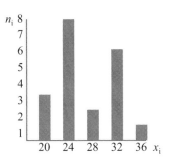

95 $\overline{x} = 38.5$ $Me = 38.5$ $Mo = 37$

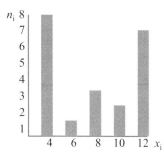

96 $\overline{x} = 7.905$ $Me = 8$ $Mo = 4$

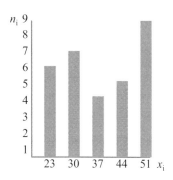

97 $\overline{x} = 37.903$ $Me = 37$ $Mo = 51$

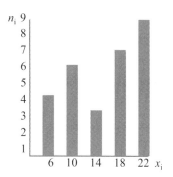

98 $\overline{x} = 15.517$ $Me = 18$ $Mo = 22$

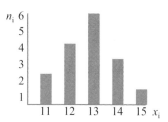

99 $\overline{x} = 12.813$ $Me = 13$ $Mo = 13$

100 $\bar{x} = 11.476$ $Me = 13$ $Mo = 13$

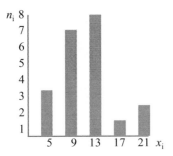

101 $\bar{x} = 37.474$ $Me = 40$ $Mo = 40$

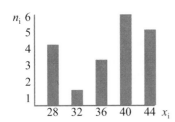

102 $\bar{x} = 14.154$ $Me = 12$ $Mo = 0$

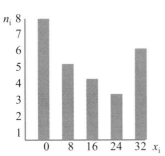

103 $\bar{x} = 30.136$ $Me = 30$ $Mo = 30$

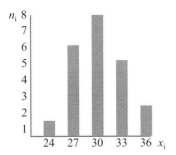

104 $\bar{x} = 41.72$ $Me = 43$ $Mo = 27$

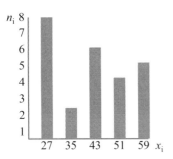

105 $\overline{x} = 16.08$ $Me = 18$ $Mo = 24$

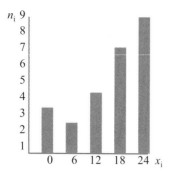

106 $\overline{x} = 10.261$ $Me = 10$ $Mo = 10$

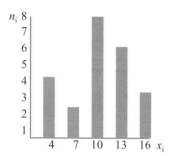

107 $\overline{x} = 49.913$ $Me = 44$ $Mo = 36$

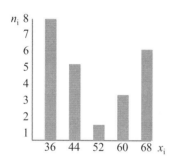

108 $\overline{x} = 32.714$ $Me = 30$ $Mo = 26$

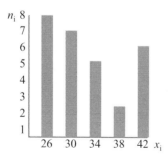

109 $\overline{x} = 35.357$ $Me = 33$ $Mo = 33$

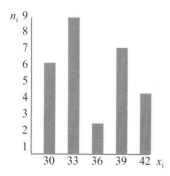

110 $\overline{x} = 44.886$ $Me = 49$ $Mo = 49$

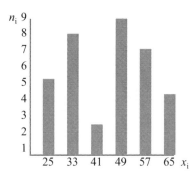

111 $\overline{x} = 49.132$ $Me = 46$ $Mo = 39$

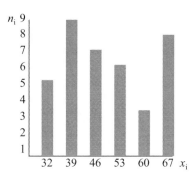

112 $\overline{x} = 27.778$ $Me = 26$ $Mo = 32$

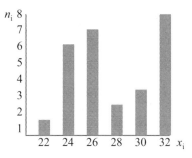

113 $\overline{x} = 6.711$ $Me = 6$ $Mo = 0$

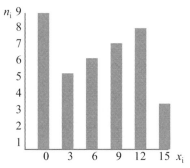

114 $\overline{x} = 9.037$ $Me = 8$ $Mo = 4$

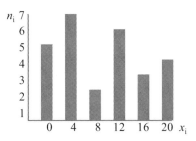

81

115 $\bar{x} = 43.75$ $Me = 39$ $Mo = 39$

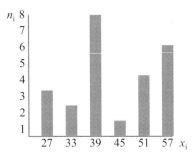

116 $\bar{x} = 11.478$ $Me = 12$ $Mo = 12$

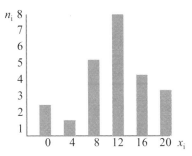

117 $\bar{x} = 4.541$ $Me = 4$ $Mo = 0$

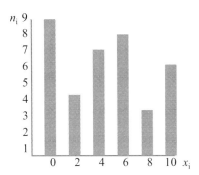

118 $\bar{x} = 37.516$ $Me = 38$ $Mo = 38$

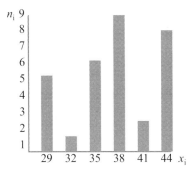

119 $\bar{x} = 37.273$ $Me = 38$ $Mo = 26$

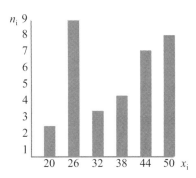

120 $\overline{x} = 25.615$ $Me = 36$ $Mo = 36$

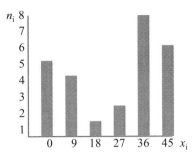

121 $\overline{x} = 4.545$ $Me = 4$ $Mo = 2$

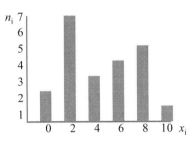

122 $\overline{x} = 30.739$ $Me = 31$ $Mo = 25$

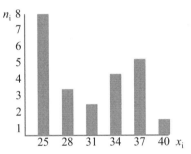

123 $\overline{x} = 28.639$ $Me = 26$ $Mo = 21$

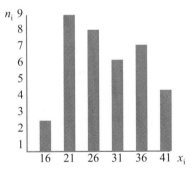

124 $\overline{x} = 46.5$ $Me = 46.5$ $Mo = 44$

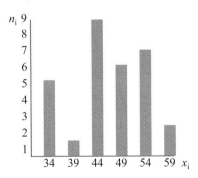

125 $\overline{x} = 49.097$ $Me = 52$ $Mo = 61$

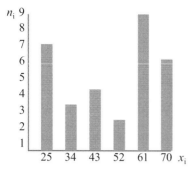

126 $\overline{x} = 15.714$ $Me = 16$ $Mo = 0$

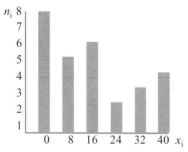

127 $\overline{x} = 43$ $Me = 42$ $Mo = 62$

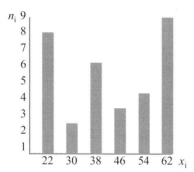

128 $\overline{x} = 44.194$ $Me = 40$ $Mo = 40$

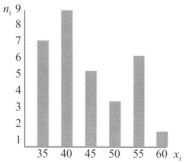

129 $\overline{x} = 44.886$ $Me = 49$ $Mo = 49$

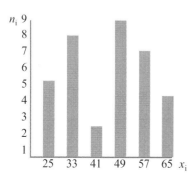

130 $\bar{x} = 49.132$ $Me = 46$ $Mo = 39$

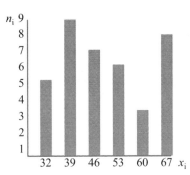

131 $\bar{x} = 25.25$ $Me = 26$ $Mo = 26$ $\sigma = 1.561$ $DM = 1.344$ $CV = 6.18\,\%$

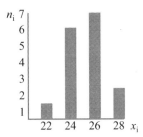

132 $\bar{x} = 21.957$ $Me = 23$ $Mo = 23$ $\sigma = 2.274$ $DM = 2.049$ $CV = 10.36\,\%$

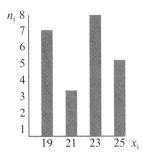

133 $\bar{x} = 18.783$ $Me = 18$ $Mo = 27$ $\sigma = 7.923$ $DM = 6.431$ $CV = 42.18\,\%$

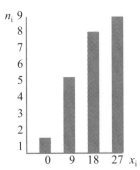

134 $\bar{x} = 24.5$ $Me = 22$ $Mo = 22$ $\sigma = 9.394$ $DM = 8.056$ $CV = 38.34\,\%$

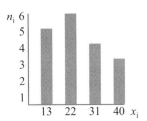

135 $\bar{x} = 12$ $Me = 13.5$ $Mo = 0$ $\sigma = 10.817$ $DM = 10$ $CV = 90.14\%$

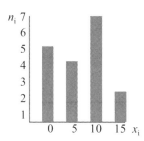

136 $\bar{x} = 6.667$ $Me = 7.5$ $Mo = 10$ $\sigma = 5$ $DM = 4.444$ $CV = 75\%$

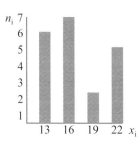

137 $\bar{x} = 16.9$ $Me = 16$ $Mo = 16$ $\sigma = 3.434$ $DM = 2.97$ $CV = 20.32\%$

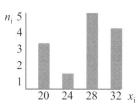

138 $\bar{x} = 27.077$ $Me = 28$ $Mo = 28$ $\sigma = 4.48$ $DM = 3.74$ $CV = 16.55\%$

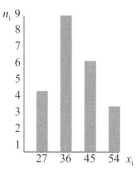

139 $\bar{x} = 39.273$ $Me = 36$ $Mo = 36$ $\sigma = 8.384$ $DM = 7.14$ $CV = 21.35\%$

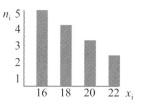

140 $\bar{x} = 18.286$ $Me = 18$ $Mo = 16$ $\sigma = 2.119$ $DM = 1.796$ $CV = 11.59\%$

141 $\bar{x} = 15$ $Me = 16$ $Mo = 16$ $\sigma = 3.317$ $DM = 2.889$ $CV = 22.11\%$

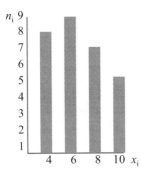

142 $\bar{x} = 6.621$ $Me = 6$ $Mo = 6$ $\sigma = 2.108$ $DM = 1.831$ $CV = 31.83\%$

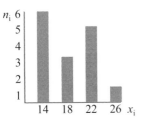

143 $\bar{x} = 18.267$ $Me = 18$ $Mo = 14$ $\sigma = 3.991$ $DM = 3.52$ $CV = 21.85\%$

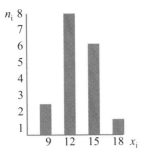

144 $\bar{x} = 13.059$ $Me = 12$ $Mo = 12$ $\sigma = 2.287$ $DM = 1.952$ $CV = 17.52\%$

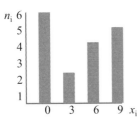

145 $\bar{x} = 4.412$ $Me = 6$ $Mo = 0$ $\sigma = 3.727$ $DM = 3.446$ $CV = 84.47\%$

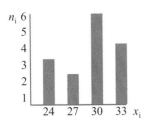

146 $\bar{x} = 29.2$ $Me = 30$ $Mo = 30$ $\sigma = 3.187$ $DM = 2.667$ $CV = 10.92\%$

147 $\bar{x} = 31.4$ $Me = 32$ $Mo = 32$ $\sigma = 4.964$ $DM = 4.016$ $CV = 15.81\ \%$

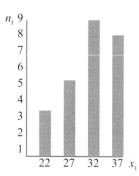

148 $\bar{x} = 25.368$ $Me = 25$ $Mo = 18$ $\sigma = 8.021$ $DM = 6.438$ $CV = 31.62\ \%$

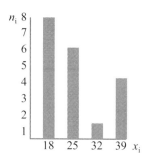

149 $\bar{x} = 40.4$ $Me = 38$ $Mo = 30$ $\sigma = 10.763$ $DM = 10.08$ $CV = 26.64\ \%$

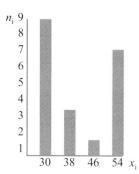

150 $\bar{x} = 8.667$ $Me = 7$ $Mo = 0$ $\sigma = 8.882$ $DM = 8.063$ $CV = 102.48\ \%$

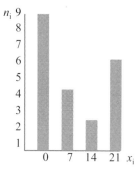

151 $\bar{x} = 16.348$ $Me = 14$ $Mo = 8$ $\sigma = 7.452$ $DM = 6.828$ $CV = 45.58\ \%$

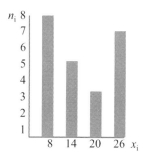

152 $\overline{x} = 10.5$ $Me = 12$ $Mo = 12$ $\sigma = 5.652$ $DM = 4.8$ $CV = 53.83\,\%$

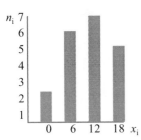

153 $\overline{x} = 39.955$ $Me = 37.5$ $Mo = 33$ $\sigma = 9.373$ $DM = 8.591$ $CV = 23.46\,\%$

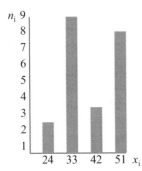

154 $\overline{x} = 40.3$ $Me = 41$ $Mo = 48$ $\sigma = 7.308$ $DM = 6.44$ $CV = 18.13\,\%$

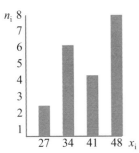

155 $\overline{x} = 15.6$ $Me = 14$ $Mo = 14$ $\sigma = 4.63$ $DM = 3.733$ $CV = 29.68\,\%$

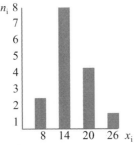

156 $\overline{x} = 2.5$ $Me = 2$ $Mo = 0$ $\sigma = 2.179$ $DM = 1.95$ $CV = 87.18\,\%$

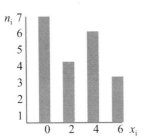

157 $\overline{x} = 16.5$ $Me = 17$ $Mo = 17$ $\sigma = 4.717$ $DM = 3.7$ $CV = 28.59\,\%$

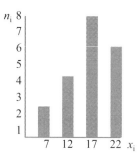

158 $\overline{x} = 5.333$ $Me = 4$ $Mo = 8$ $\sigma = 3.343$ $DM = 2.921$ $CV = 62.68\,\%$

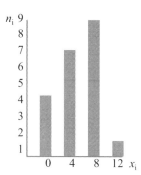

159 $\overline{x} = 3.938$ $Me = 4.5$ $Mo = 0$ $\sigma = 3.473$ $DM = 3.188$ $CV = 88.19\,\%$

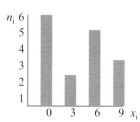

160 $\overline{x} = 24.682$ $Me = 24$ $Mo = 21$ $\sigma = 3.495$ $DM = 3.198$ $CV = 14.16\,\%$

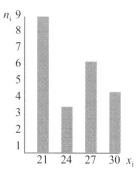

161 $\overline{x} = 14.28$ $Me = 13$ $Mo = 17$ $\sigma = 4.035$ $DM = 3.571$ $CV = 28.26\,\%$

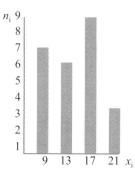

162 $\overline{x} = 37.087$ $Me = 35$ $Mo = 27$ $\sigma = 9.5$ $DM = 8.287$ $CV = 25.62\,\%$

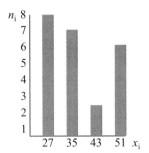

163 $\overline{x} = 9.6$ $Me = 6$ $Mo = 6$ $\sigma = 5.817$ $DM = 5.16$ $CV = 60.6\,\%$

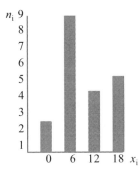

164 $\overline{x} = 4.375$ $Me = 4$ $Mo = 2$ $\sigma = 2.666$ $DM = 2.32$ $CV = 60.94\,\%$

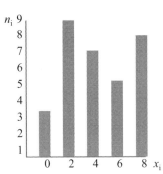

165 $\overline{x} = 4.316$ $Me = 4$ $Mo = 4$ $\sigma = 2.848$ $DM = 2.294$ $CV = 65.99\,\%$

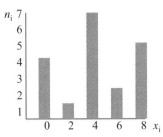

166 $\overline{x} = 16.828$ $Me = 16$ $Mo = 32$ $\sigma = 11.573$ $DM = 9.855$ $CV = 68.77\,\%$

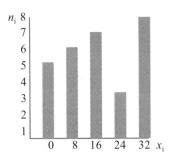

167 $\bar{x} = 19.667$ $Me = 20$ $Mo = 0$ $\sigma = 15.38$ $DM = 13.711$ $CV = 78.21\ \%$

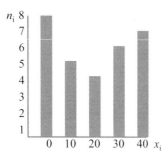

168 $\bar{x} = 41.13$ $Me = 42$ $Mo = 32$ $\sigma = 8.295$ $DM = 7.429$ $CV = 20.17\ \%$

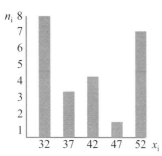

169 $\bar{x} = 26.182$ $Me = 26$ $Mo = 26$ $\sigma = 2.757$ $DM = 2.27$ $CV = 10.53\ \%$

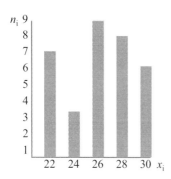

170 $\bar{x} = 15.692$ $Me = 18$ $Mo = 24$ $\sigma = 7.994$ $DM = 6.994$ $CV = 50.94\ \%$

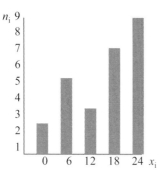

171 $\bar{x} = 46.481$ $Me = 45$ $Mo = 50$ $\sigma = 6.209$ $DM = 5.24$ $CV = 13.36\ \%$

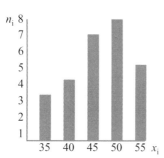

172 $\bar{x} = 31.667$ $Me = 33$ $Mo = 17$ $\sigma = 11.926$ $DM = 10.333$ $CV = 37.66\%$

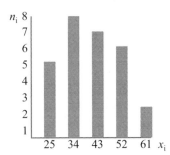

173 $\bar{x} = 40.429$ $Me = 43$ $Mo = 34$ $\sigma = 10.719$ $DM = 9.184$ $CV = 26.51\%$

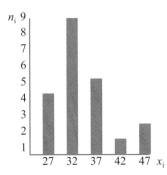

174 $\bar{x} = 34.143$ $Me = 32$ $Mo = 32$ $\sigma = 5.684$ $DM = 4.558$ $CV = 16.65\%$

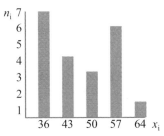

175 $\bar{x} = 46.667$ $Me = 43$ $Mo = 36$ $\sigma = 9.321$ $DM = 8.508$ $CV = 19.97\%$

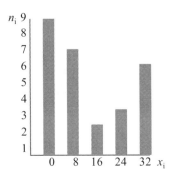

176 $\bar{x} = 13.037$ $Me = 8$ $Mo = 0$ $\sigma = 12.536$ $DM = 11.303$ $CV = 96.16\%$

177 $x = 37.379$ $Me = 36$ $Mo = 28$ $\sigma = 10.727$ $DM = 9.341$ $CV = 28.7\,\%$

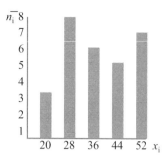

178 $\overline{x} = 30.071$ $Me = 31$ $Mo = 31$ $\sigma = 2.59$ $DM = 2.27$ $CV = 8.61\,\%$

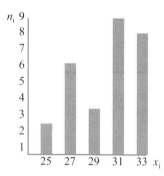

179 $\overline{x} = 21.44$ $Me = 24$ $Mo = 24$ $\sigma = 5.756$ $DM = 4.992$ $CV = 26.84\,\%$

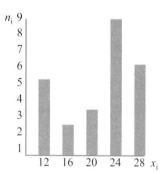

180 $\overline{x} = 16.294$ $Me = 17$ $Mo = 11$ $\sigma = 4.991$ $DM = 4.63$ $CV = 30.63\,\%$

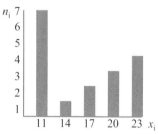

181 $\overline{x} = 27.667$ $Me = 26$ $Mo = 22$ $\sigma = 5.406$ $DM = 4.611$ $CV = 19.54\,\%$

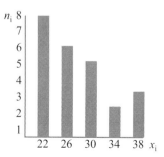

182 $\bar{x} = 50.25$ $Me = 48$ $Mo = 48$ $\sigma = 11.691$ $DM = 9.804$ $CV = 23.27\%$

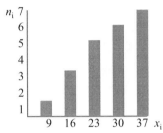

183 $\bar{x} = 27.773$ $Me = 30$ $Mo = 37$ $\sigma = 8.279$ $DM = 7.087$ $CV = 29.81\%$

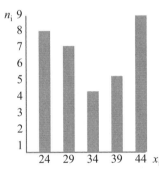

184 $\bar{x} = 34$ $Me = 34$ $Mo = 44$ $\sigma = 7.785$ $DM = 6.97$ $CV = 22.9\%$

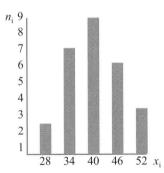

185 $\bar{x} = 40.222$ $Me = 40$ $Mo = 40$ $\sigma = 6.63$ $DM = 5.185$ $CV = 16.48\%$

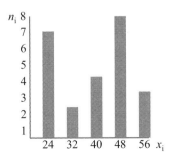

186 $\bar{x} = 39.333$ $Me = 40$ $Mo = 48$ $\sigma = 11.528$ $DM = 10.167$ $CV = 29.31\%$

187 $\bar{x} = 10$ $Me = 10$ $Mo = 15$ $\sigma = 6$ $DM = 5.2$ $CV = 60\,\%$

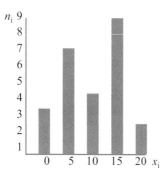

188 $\bar{x} = 24.421$ $Me = 27$ $Mo = 27$ $\sigma = 9.692$ $DM = 8.144$ $CV = 39.69\,\%$

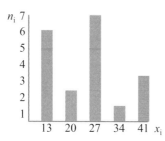

189 $\bar{x} = 27.31$ $Me = 27$ $Mo = 28$ $\sigma = 1.262$ $DM = 1.08$ $CV = 4.62\,\%$

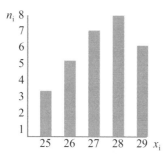

190 $\bar{x} = 1.952$ $Me = 2$ $Mo = 2$ $\sigma = 1.174$ $DM = 0.921$ $CV = 60.14\,\%$

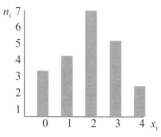

191 $\bar{x} = 30.429$ $Me = 29$ $Mo = 29$ $\sigma = 11.525$ $DM = 9.633$ $CV = 37.87\,\%$

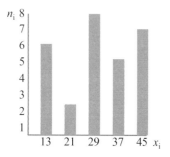

192 $\overline{x} = 36.538$ $Me = 36$ $Mo = 40$ $\sigma = 2.912$ $DM = 2.621$ $CV = 7.97\%$

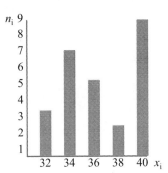

193 $\overline{x} = 42.391$ $Me = 39$ $Mo = 33$ $\sigma = 8.453$ $DM = 7.713$ $CV = 19.94\%$

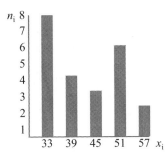

194 $\overline{x} = 43.308$ $Me = 44$ $Mo = 41$ $\sigma = 7.819$ $DM = 6.462$ $CV = 18.05\%$

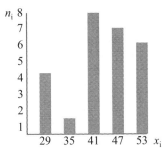

195 $\overline{x} = 10.25$ $Me = 11$ $Mo = 8$ $\sigma = 3.128$ $DM = 2.625$ $CV = 30.52\%$

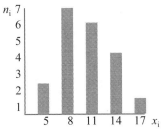

196 $\overline{x} = 36.286$ $Me = 34$ $Mo = 31$ $\sigma = 4.802$ $DM = 4.395$ $CV = 13.23\%$

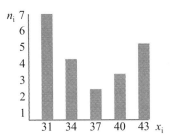

197 $\bar{x} = 32.043$ $Me = 39$ $Mo = 39$ $\sigma = 12.551$ $DM = 11.342$ $CV = 39.17\,\%$

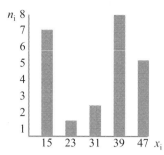

198 $\bar{x} = 26.824$ $Me = 28$ $Mo = 28$ $\sigma = 3.148$ $DM = 2.727$ $CV = 11.74\,\%$

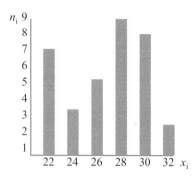

199 $\bar{x} = 47.438$ $Me = 48$ $Mo = 48$ $\sigma = 10.213$ $DM = 8.273$ $CV = 21.53\,\%$

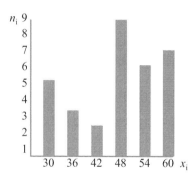

200 $\bar{x} = 28.824$ $Me = 29$ $Mo = 31$ $\sigma = 1.79$ $DM = 1.599$ $CV = 6.21\,\%$

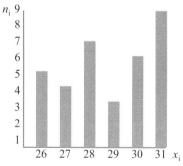

201 $\bar{x} = 39.538$ $Me = 40$ $Mo = 46$ $\sigma = 5.286$ $DM = 4.568$ $CV = 13.37\,\%$

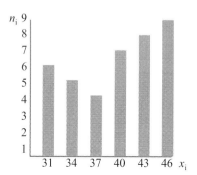

202 $\bar{x} = 37.679$ $Me = 35$ $Mo = 35$ $\sigma = 6.877$ $DM = 5.727$ $CV = 18.25\,\%$

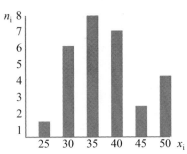

203 $\bar{x} = 10.839$ $Me = 12$ $Mo = 20$ $\sigma = 8.012$ $DM = 7.284$ $CV = 73.92\,\%$

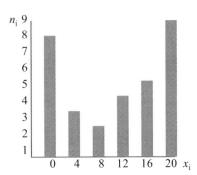

204 $\bar{x} = 48.333$ $Me = 51$ $Mo = 51$ $\sigma = 10.812$ $DM = 9.444$ $CV = 22.37\,\%$

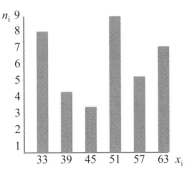

205 $\bar{x} = 31.529$ $Me = 32$ $Mo = 16$ $\sigma = 13.007$ $DM = 10.879$ $CV = 41.25\,\%$

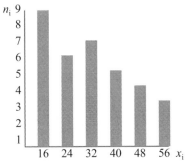

206 $\bar{x} = 25.794$ $Me = 25$ $Mo = 19$ $\sigma = 5.161$ $DM = 4.37$ $CV = 20.01\,\%$

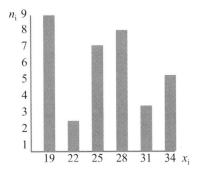

207 $\bar{x} = 37.308$ $Me = 40$ $Mo = 45$ $\sigma = 7.236$ $DM = 6.361$ $CV = 19.4\,\%$

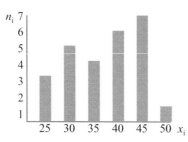

208 $\bar{x} = 31.889$ $Me = 33$ $Mo = 23$ $\sigma = 8.507$ $DM = 7.623$ $CV = 26.68\,\%$

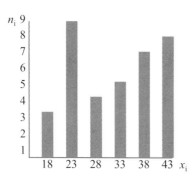

209 $\bar{x} = 9$ $Me = 10$ $Mo = 10$ $\sigma = 8$ $DM = 6.32$ $CV = 88.89\,\%$

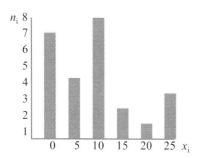

210 $\bar{x} = 41.25$ $Me = 43$ $Mo = 55$ $\sigma = 14.316$ $DM = 13.25$ $CV = 34.7\,\%$

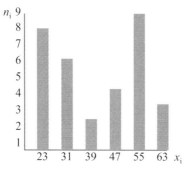

211 $\bar{x} = 15.522$ $Me = 14$ $Mo = 7$ $\sigma = 11.669$ $DM = 10.242$ $CV = 75.18\,\%$

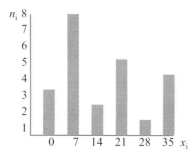

212 $\bar{x} = 55.273$ $Me = 56$ $Mo = 56$ $\sigma = 11.876$ $DM = 9.697$ $CV = 21.49\%$

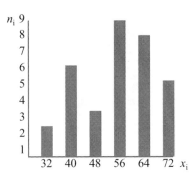

213 $\bar{x} = 22.966$ $Me = 27$ $Mo = 27$ $\sigma = 13.071$ $DM = 11.279$ $CV = 56.92\%$

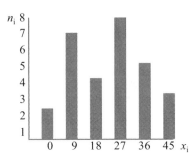

214 $\bar{x} = 12.125$ $Me = 10$ $Mo = 10$ $\sigma = 4.781$ $DM = 4.052$ $CV = 39.43\%$

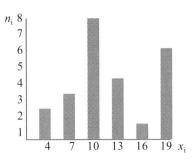

215 $\bar{x} = 25.741$ $Me = 26$ $Mo = 27$ $\sigma = 1.734$ $DM = 1.602$ $CV = 6.74\%$

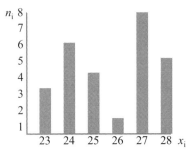

216 $\bar{x} = 57.75$ $Me = 62$ $Mo = 70$ $\sigma = 14.14$ $DM = 12.781$ $CV = 24.48\%$

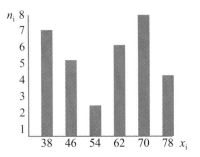

217 $\bar{x} = 29.091$ $Me = 30$ $Mo = 30$ $\sigma = 16.023$ $DM = 13.278$ $CV = 55.08\,\%$

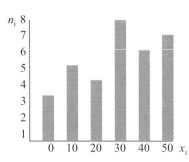

218 $\bar{x} = 47.026$ $Me = 43$ $Mo = 25$ $\sigma = 16.736$ $DM = 15.133$ $CV = 35.59\,\%$

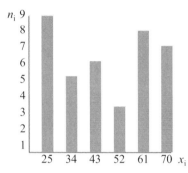

219 $\bar{x} = 23.742$ $Me = 23$ $Mo = 23$ $\sigma = 1.645$ $DM = 1.476$ $CV = 6.93\,\%$

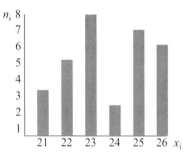

220 $\bar{x} = 36$ $Me = 38$ $Mo = 38$ $\sigma = 3.408$ $DM = 2.968$ $CV = 9.47\,\%$

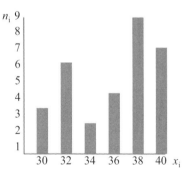

221 $\bar{x} = 37.857$ $Me = 36$ $Mo = 34$ $\sigma = 6.632$ $DM = 5.571$ $CV = 17.52\,\%$

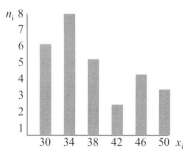

222 $\bar{x} = 29.818$ $Me = 29$ $Mo = 23$ $\sigma = 5.638$ $DM = 5.207$ $CV = 18.91\,\%$

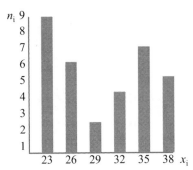

223 $\bar{x} = 19.267$ $Me = 23$ $Mo = 23$ $\sigma = 6.767$ $DM = 5.849$ $CV = 35.12\,\%$

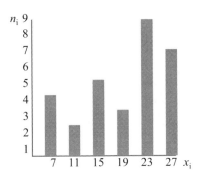

224 $\bar{x} = 31.848$ $Me = 31$ $Mo = 35$ $\sigma = 5.721$ $DM = 4.753$ $CV = 17.96\,\%$

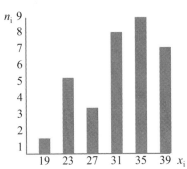

225 $\bar{x} = 24.034$ $Me = 23$ $Mo = 20$ $\sigma = 3.961$ $DM = 3.417$ $CV = 16.48\,\%$

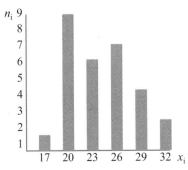

226 $\bar{x} = 53.261$ $Me = 53$ $Mo = 65$ $\sigma = 10.975$ $DM = 9.164$ $CV = 20.61\,\%$

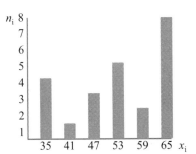

227 $\bar{x} = 12.828$ $Me = 12$ $Mo = 0$ $\sigma = 10.999$ $DM = 9.603$ $CV = 85.74\,\%$

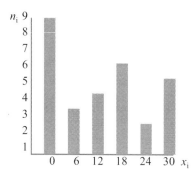

228 $\bar{x} = 21.882$ $Me = 20$ $Mo = 40$ $\sigma = 14.56$ $DM = 13.412$ $CV = 66.54\,\%$

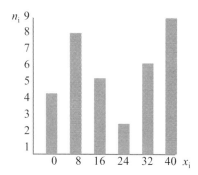

229 $\bar{x} = 20.621$ $Me = 14$ $Mo = 14$ $\sigma = 11.068$ $DM = 9.874$ $CV = 53.68\,\%$

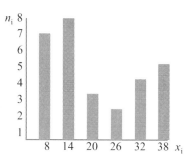

Made in United States
Orlando, FL
28 December 2024